CHAPTER 1

INTRODUCTION

The United States is currently grappling with the challenge of attempting to effect a major reduction in the military establishment while preserving adequate strength to protect its national interests and fulfill its international commitments. With the first cracks in the Iron Curtain, many sectors in American society began to clamor for a "peace dividend," or a dramatic shift in dollars and national resources away from defense programs towards domestic social spending. It was confidently expected that with the West's main rival in decline, international military tensions would rapidly dissipate. The dissolution of the Soviet Union, however, resulted in a significantly more complex and amorphous set of security issues for the United States.

Since December 1989, US forces have been almost continuously engaged in hostilities, of greater or lesser intensity, in several areas of the world simultaneously. These include a major war in the Persian Gulf, a full-scale invasion of the Panamanian isthmus, and a host of fluctuating commitments to peacekeeping, peace making, and humanitarian operations from Somalia to Bosnia, and many lesser conflicts in between. Despite this brisk operational tempo and the continuing deterioration of international stability, a primary preoccupation of the Executive Branch and Congress has been the decrement of the Defense Department and a significant realignment of the military's force structure.

These proposed reductions and realignments inevitably spawn fierce political debate between conservative and liberal factions about the role and function of the military in our society. A key subordinate issue in this debate is the establishment of a balanced force structure that effectively and efficiently divides responsibilities and assigns forces between Active Duty (Regular) Army and Reserve Component (primarily National Guard) Army forces. Many of these issues go to the very heart of the contending factions most basic ideological beliefs.

At times, the seemingly dogmatic adherence to these sometimes archaic ideological tenants can seem to defy rational analysis. Many individual's extreme commitment to the dogmas of their political ideology supersede any pragmatic consideration of the threat. The influence of these ideologies often causes the debate to assume a fiercely partisan and emotional tone, and as often as not, fosters a climate of mutual hostility that blocks rational, or productive, compromise.

While perhaps unique within the last forty years, the effort to dramatically reduce and realign defense capability in the face of clear and present dangers to the national interest is not unprecedented in American history. To a remarkable degree the current debates mirror those of the Federalists and Anti-Federalists on this same subject in the 1780-90s.

The struggle to create a permanent American military establishment began concurrently with the formation of the American Government after the end of the Revolutionary War in 1783. It continued through the ratification of the Constitution in 1788 and did not assume a shape recognizable to the modern eye until early in the Jefferson administration in 1801. These debates solidified two distinctly American theories of national defense, one republican, and

2

one federalist whose ideological tenants still animate and influence discussion of defense issues to our own time. Despite their central importance in defining the role and function of the US Army in American society, however, these early debates are seldom accurately alluded to in framing the current discussions.

In this thesis I will explore the following research question: Do the parallels between the debates on the proposed downsizing of the United States Armed Forces in the 1990s and the debates on the creation of a permanent American military establishment in the 1780s and 90s indicate the continuing influence of identifiable republican/ liberal, or federalist/conservative political ideologies? The subordinate questions to be addressed are:

1. What were/are the debates?

2. Are there valid parallels?

3. What were the historic military consequences of the ideological influences and compromises?

4. Can an understanding of the historical origins of these ideologies and the ways in which they continue to influence the debate offer useful insights for designing compromises that are both politically acceptable, and militarily sound?

The thesis is organized into an introduction, five intermediate chapters, and a conclusion.

Chapter 1 is the introduction and sets forth the research questions, the scope of the thesis, and some basic definitional terminology.

Chapter 2 will provide an overview important historical background information in order to place the political debates and military events into the proper 18th century context. It will also explore the military origins of the schism between the federalists and republicans during and after the Revolution.

Chapter 3 will provide a detailed explanation of the origins of American liberal ideology in the 17th and 18th century European Enlightenment experience. It will also examine the influence of British liberal political historiography on American revolutionary thought.

Chapter 4 examines the military establishment debates of the 1780s in detail, and places special emphasis on the evolution and rationale behind the contradictory military clauses of the U.S. Constitution. It also delineates the origins and nature of the ideological schism which ultimately resulted in the division of the American revolutionary leadership into two conflicting political parties.

Chapter 5 provides a detailed account of the "peace establishment" debates of the 1790s and traces the evolution of the the permanent American military until 1800.

Chapter 6 gives a brief summary of the evolution of the American military establishment in the 20th century, and then examines the parallels in the modern defense debates with those of the 18th century.

Chapter 7, the concluding chapter, presents a synopsis of the historical influence of political ideology on defense policy, and discusses the ways in which an appreciation of the nature and origin of these ideologies can yield practical information in designing effective compromises.

I am a regular Field Artillery officer with 13 years' experience in a variety of troop and headquarter units. While never having been assigned directly to a readiness position, I have some experience in working with Guard and Reserve forces in Divisions with a round-out component. During Operation Desert Shield/Storm, I worked extensively with Guard and Reserve Officers who were detailed to the Pentagon's Army Operations Center.

I have an abiding personal interest in military history and have read extensively on the subject of wartime operations. In the last several years I have become increasingly interested in the historic social and political traditions which dominate our peacetime military posture. I have grown concerned that in our zeal to promote military efficiency, many officers on both sides of the Regular Army-National Guard debate have fallen into dogmatic mind sets, and, in framing their proposals, do not take into account the historic role of both military components in American society. I hope that a demonstration of the similarities between the debates of the founding fathers, and the current debates will help put the arguments into perspective and offer useful insights in the development of an effectively balanced force.

A note on terminology: This paper concerns itself first and foremost with the origin, development, and continuing influence of pro and anti-military political ideology. Historian Lawrence Cress developed the most helpful definition of ideology I discovered while researching this paper. I offer Dr. Cress's most salient observations on the meaning of ideology so that there will be minimal confusion with the use of this term in the body of the text:

> Ideology is distinct from valid fact. An ideology is a coherent (though not necessarily consistent) system of "distorted ideas" which purports to be factual and carries with it a more or less explicit evaluation of the "facts." Ideology mobilizes public opinion by articulating and fusing into effective formulations opinions and attitudes that are other wise too scattered and vague to be acted upon.[1]

In the course of this thesis, I will be discussing the military organizations of the early United States and their equivalents in the 1990s. In general terms these will be defined as:

Militia. The armed citizenry grouped into a military force that is not part of a regular or standing establishment, and that is subject to be called into service in an emergency.

National Guard. The military reserve units controlled by each state, equipped by the federal government, and subject to the call of either the federal or state government.

Regular Troops. Composed of long service (professional) soldiers organized into more or less permanently standing units under the discipline, direction, and control of the central, as opposed to the state, government.

In the 18th century there was also another type of military grouping, "volunteer" organizations raised and supported by the various states. The title volunteer conveyed a precise shade of meaning distinct from the general term militia, which was important in determining the organization's legal status and its relationship to other units. Arguably, volunteers can be viewed as a subset of the militia because generally speaking the volunteers were drawn from the same pool of manpower that would ordinarily have been subject to standard militia employment.

Often these volunteers would be younger members of the community, perhaps in search of a little adventure before settling down to life in a agricultural village. They were also sometimes drawn from those in need of the extra cash brought in by participating in a particular extended operation. Occasionally they were more or less professional frontiersmen and soldiers hired to provide a screening force against Indian incursions by ranging (hence the term "Ranger") between outposts.

For the broad purposes of this thesis, however, 18th century military organizations can be divided into two expansive categories: Units composed of essentially part-time "citizen" soldiers grouped

6

under the broad category of militia and units comprised of full-time professional soldiers enlisted in, or assigned to, the regular federal service for long periods of time. In this paper, volunteers will be generally included in whichever category to which their conditions of service obligation were most analogous.

When discussing the dichotomy between minimally disciplined, loosely organized, and semi-trained forces, such as characterized the vast majority of militia and volunteers, and highly disciplined, organized, and well-drilled troops, such as ideally constitute a regular establishment, interposing a third category creates unnecessary confusion. For the sake of this comparison, suffice it to argue that those long-serving and disciplined volunteer units in the wars of the 18th century had, for all intents and purposes, become indistinguishable with regular troops.

In spirit, the modern Army National Guardsmen are the inheritors of the American militia tradition. Indeed, under Title 10 of the United States Code: "the National Guard is the organized militia of the United States."[2] Though changed dramatically by the evolution of the relationship between the Federal Government and the individual states and by modern concepts of organization and training, the National Guard still fulfills the role of the part-time, community based, citizen soldier. Furthermore, the National Guard still performs domestic missions at the orders of the State Governor. As numerous events in recent years have demonstrated, the issue of the preeminence of Federal over state authority to command the Guard remains very much a matter of political controversy.

As in the 18th century, there is currently a third category of military organization; The Army Reserve. The Army Reserve is exclusively controlled by the Department of the Army, but it is also composed of part-time, essentially "citizen," soldiers. The modern

National Guard and Army Reserve have distinctly different statutory functions, but are united under the catch phrase, "Reserve Component." In the minds of those arguing for the economic and philosophic advantages of a "part-time" military, the two are effectively synonymous. In an effort to avoid confusion caused by jargon, and because the term "National Guard" contains an evocative resonance better suited to the hypothesis of this thesis, I will use the term National Guard exclusively unless the distinction between the two organizations is directly relevant.

This work will draw extensively from eighteenth century political pamphlets, newspaper editorials, letters, and other period materials. In the eighteenth century the rules of usage, spelling, grammar, and capitalization were considerably less rigid than in the present day. Within the body of a quote, I will generally use the spelling and composition as it appeared in the original material, unless such usage would confuse the meaning of the writer.

This scope of this study is limited to the influence of political ideology on American defense policy. Certainly other factors have also exhibited a major influence on the development of the military establishment. Chief among these are the state of the nation's finances. Within the limits set for this paper it would be impossible to do justice to the complex issue of American finances, therefore I have included this subject only where its influence was directly relevant to that of political ideology. This is in no way intended to mitigate the importance of this subject, but is a device for maintaining a sharp focus for the thesis.

CHAPTER 2

HISTORICAL OVERVIEW

The Colonial Militia Heritage and the English Civil War:

The British colonists who first founded and settled the colonies of North America found themselves surrounded by an often hostile population of Native Americans who's land they were usurping. Though chartered and nominally sponsored by the British Crown, they were expected to be self-supporting and self-defending. The colonies' chronic shortage of manpower, and marginal economic condition, however, made the hiring of professional soldiers for colony defense out of the question.[1] Furthermore, these colonists were the inheritors of the strong English militia tradition, the basis of which was the concept of universal military service for able bodied males.

While minor details of age and frequency of service varied from colony to colony, all American colonial governments stipulated some form of military obligation in their basic laws.[2] During the first century of colonial settlement, Indian conflicts were frequent, and the requirement to keep and remain proficient with arms was reinforced by periodic duty on active service. Militia laws were enforced; attendance at the periodic militia assemblies and drills was taken seriously; and the colonies generally maintained forces capable of coping with the level of threat posed by Indians or rival European colonies.

As the expansion of the colonies pushed the frontier further from the original settlements, however, people in the older towns and cities along the coasts took the militia obligation less seriously.

Drills were infrequent, and the penalties for failing to maintain proper arms and accouterments were less stringently enforced. One can imagine that the incentive for the average eastern farmer to maintain expensive arms and equipment against an increasingly improbable threat was minimal. Occasionally, clerical or other leaders would thunder about the need to "reform" the militia and would cite failure to comply with the militia laws as an example of nascent decadence creeping into colonial life.[3] Nonetheless, many citizens continued to shirk their military responsibilities. Gradually, the militia organizations in the larger towns began to take on the form (and exclusiveness) of fraterna. organizations.[4]

The unique nature of Indian fighting in North America also had an impact on both the types of arms favored by the colonists and their manner of drill. Weapons and drill formations suited to the battlefields of Europe, were of only limited utility in Indian fighting. Swords were elegant, but expensive, and took years of training to master. A hatchet or tomahawk could be equally effective in a frontier melee and was a useful farm tool as well.[5] Rigidly linear formations and elaborate drill were impossible to maintain in closely forested terrain and were increasingly abandoned in favor of open order skirmishing and reliance on aimed marksmanship. Frontier colonial methods of warfare became steadily less influenced by Europe and progressively adapted themselves to the nature of the available manpower and to the irregular tactics of the Indian threat.

Seventeenth Century events in the New World were also unfolding against the backdrop of the English Civil War, the military dictatorship of Oliver Cromwell, and the restoration of the monarchy. Many American colonists were initially approving and supportive of the Parliamentary rebellion against Charles I. This was especially true in

10

heavily puritan New England. By and large, though, the Americans were alarmed and were greatly disappointed when the professional Army, raised, trained, and organized by Cromwell, suspended parliamentary liberty and established military rule.

Philosophically, the military dictatorship imposed by Cromwell was the seminal event for American Englishmen in the 17th Century, and was a key element in the reflexive distrust of professional standing armies that became a guiding tenant of radical whig ideology in the 1700s.

The Enlightenment and the American Military Experience:

It would be difficult to overstate the influence of the Enlightenment on the leaders of the American Revolution. English political philosopher John Locke's dictum that rulers divine their authority from the consent of the governed and French philosopher Jean Jacques Rousseau's concept of the "Social Contract" were fundamental to the framing of coherent political objection to the real and imagined grievances of the colonies against the crown.

Within the context of Enlightenment political philosophy, the political coup d'etat committed by Cromwell's New Model Army seemed a predictable and inevitable corruption of unrestricted power: "tyranny" in the argot of the times. It was taken as an unquestioned article of faith by American intellectuals that "power corrupts, and absolute power corrupts absolutely."[6] In their minds there could be no more tangible manifestation of corrupt power than a standing professional army. This inherent prejudice was reinforced by the negative experiences of the colonials with British regular troops during the first half of the 18th century and especially in the French and Indian (Seven Years) War.

The colonial military leaders deeply resented the arrogance and contemptuous attitude that many regular British officers exhibited towards the American militia. The defeats of Braddock and other British commanders, blundering by their failure to heed the sound advice of American frontiersmen with years of practical Indian fighting experience, further eroded the colonials respect and regard for the professional abilities of the British regulars. The British, for their part, were equally dismayed and infuriated by the unmilitary conduct, presumption, and disorder of the average colonial militiaman. This lack of respect soon caused the British regulars to regard colonial militia as an undisciplined rabble, and they began to relegate them to the role of servile auxiliaries, further alienating the Americans.

The events of the war with France and the constant conflicts between the American frontier settlements and the Indians caused the Crown to decide, after 1763, to permanently garrison the colonies with several thousand regulars. The subsequent decision to billet them upon an unwilling civilian frontier population greatly exacerbated the tensions between the Redcoats and Americans already present as a result of the War. The presence of these troops, and the petty frictions with the locals that inevitably resulted, satisfied radical American Whigs (the opposition political party to the royalist tories) of the correctness of their ideological prejudice against regular armies, and the basically corrupting influence of these institutions. The rising American resistance to the Crown's taxation policies caused increasingly frequent clashes between crown troops and colonials.

The worst of these run-ins, the so called "Boston Massacre" in 1770, where regular British troops fired on a threatening American mob killing or wounding dozens, fueled and added momentum to the growing rift between the colonies and the mother country. Radical American Whigs were coming to regard regular British troops as an army of occupation who's purpose was to suppress the peoples liberties rather than to protect them from outside enemies. The radicals began to form secret "committees of public safety" who's purpose was to stockpile and distribute arms and to prepare the militia for the probability of hostilities with the mother country.

The Colonials began the Revolutionary War with an almost mystic faith in the abilities of militia. Heavily influenced by the radical Whig Historiography of the period, most rebel supporters believed that freemen fighting for their "sacred liberties" against the mercenaries of a tyrant would inevitably triumph. Persuaded of the unique "virtue" of the "American Race," they sought in the struggle for independence confirmation of their faith in these fundamental Enlightenment ideologies. It was commonly held among the radical pamphleteers of 1775 that what the militia lacked in training and organization would be more than adequately compensated for by their enthusiasm and numbers. A concept which the great French military philosopher of the Enlightenment Comte Jacques de Guibert envisioned as:

> A people vigorous in its genius, its resources and its government . . . in whom austere virtues and a national militia were joined to a settled policy of aggrandizement; one which did not lose sight of its purpose, which knew how to make war cheaply and to subsist on its victories . . . .[8]

Guibert despaired of such a people ever arising in corrupt old Europe, but the events of the summer of 1775 generated Whig confidence that, indeed, such a people inhabited North America. The colonial population, gripped by what Charles Royster characterized as the "Rage Militaire," poured into the rebel camps surrounding Boston, some units traveling from as far away as Virginia.[9] Confident in their cause, themselves, and the superiority of their innate virtue, the siege lines around Boston took on a rollicking holiday air. George Washington, newly appointed by the Continental Congress to command the Colonial forces surrounding Boston, despaired of ever imposing military order on the throng.

The ill-considered and badly handled British assault on Breeds Hill, and the mauling of the Crown's regulars by the American militiamen defending the earthworks there, tended to confirm rebel faith in the superiority of moral virtue over discipline and training. Lost on all but Washington and a few of the more astute American observers, however, was the fact that at the end of the day, patriot militia relinquished the field in the face of British bayonets.

The British evacuation of Boston convinced the majority of militia units that they could return to the pressing business of their farms and shops congratulating themselves on a job well done. The desperate entreaties of George Washington that the Army needed to prepare against the inevitable British counterattack fell largely on deaf ears. Lacking any real authority or power to enforce his orders, Washington stood impotent as militia came and went of their own volition. When at length the British counterattacked through New York in 1776, the militia troops suffered an unrelenting string of defeats and humiliations that came within an ace of destroying the Rebel Army. Were it not for the strategic audacity and tactical skill of Washington's Christmas assault on Trenton, the rebel cause would almost certainly have collapsed during the winter of 1777.

Washington was driven to his desperate gamble at Trenton by the impending departure of most of the militia forces on 1 January 1777. In January 1776, these militia units had been enlisted by their states for one year's duty with the "Continental" forces. With the year coming to a close they expressed a nearly universal intention to return to their homes. Despite Washington's impassioned appeals to their patriotism, and his explanations of the desperate situation of the

cause, they remained adamant in their refusal to extend their
enlistments.

The enthusiasm of the summer of 1775 had evaporated in the face
of the defeats of 1776. The pressing business of neglected farms and
shops now seemed more important than soldiering. Against the prospect
of another tortuous winter in camp and further defeat at the hands of
British regulars, even Tom Paine's superb rhetoric about the "times
that try men's souls" seemed hollow.[10] Most felt they had done their
part and it was now someone else's turn. Washington realized that if
there were to be any hope for the fledgling Republic he must win a
victory while he still had an army.

The implacable desertion of the militia in the face of grave
crisis was the pivotal experience for Washington and his principle
lieutenants in their development of an American war policy. After
Trenton and Princeton, Washington concentrated his efforts to the
maximum extent possible on the development of a purely "Continental,"
or national military organization. Despite a continuing commitment to
the general ideals of Enlightenment philosophy, many prominent
officers, such as Henry Knox, Daniel Morgan, and most importantly
Alexander Hamilton, developed a dislike and distrust of militia that
rivaled any held by a British regular officer.

They regarded with anger and resentment what they perceived to
be the undisciplined and frequently capricious behavior of the militia.
This, combined with the shortsighted and self-serving policies of many
of the state governments which controlled the citizen-soldiers,
convinced Washington's inner circle that only a large body of troops
enlisted in the national service for long periods, and subject to the
strict discipline which characterized regulars, had any hope of
prevailing over the English and Hessian troops they opposed. Over the

course of the remainder of the War Washington would clamor for more and more troops to be enlisted for long periods into the Continental regiments.

By 1782, most officers of the Continental Army would scarcely credit militia units with having any merit whatsoever. Their burning resentment toward the consistently shabby treatment accorded them by the states and the Continental Congress caused them to exaggerate the role of the continental regulars in the successful campaigns of the war, and to minimize the very real contributions of the militia units. Far from being a help, many professed to believe that militia had been a positive hindrance in the prosecution of the War.

In fact, The continental establishment never numbered above 10,000 at any time, and while they formed the disciplined, professional core around which operations were conducted, their activities would have been impossible without the mass and weight provided by the militia.[11] Properly handled, and assigned appropriate missions, the militia often acquitted itself well as the victories at Ticonderoga, Saratoga, and Kings Mountain attest. Furthermore, the militia performed the vital functions of policing and patrolling the states, and holding the American royalist Tories in check.

Despite this, many continental officers came away from the Revolution convinced that, in the frustrated wartime words of General Washington; "No militia will ever acquire the habits necessary to resist a regular force . . . ."[12] The traditional Whig intellectuals, on the other hand, saw their worst prejudices against regular establishments confirmed by the events of the "Newburgh Conspiracy," the abortive attempt by a group of continental officers to organize a mutiny against the civil government in early 1783.[13]

16

The crisis at Newburgh was a result of long festering disputes between the continental officers, Congress, and the state governments over issues of officers back-pay, pensions, other compensations for the sacrifices made by the members of the Continental Army during the War. The full extent of the conspiracy remains unknown, but almost certainly reached into the highest levels of the Congress, and the motives of many of the participants were tangled with other issues besides just compensation for military service.[14] Chief among these was the long standing enmity between Washington and his second-in-command, Horatio Gates.

Gates' jealousy, and his desire to supplant Washington as commander, were his primary motivations for inflaming the long simmering grievances of the officers at the Army's final encampment in Newburgh, New York. His attempt to usurp the loyalty of the officers, and possibly to lead them in defiance of the civil authorities, was only narrowly, and with difficulty, stopped by Washington. The part played by petty internal rivalry notwithstanding, the incident at Newburgh reawakened the deepest anxieties of the "republicans," as the followers of Jefferson and other adherents of the traditional Enlightenment ideologies were beginning to be called.

Although the Newburgh conspiracy was opposed and suppressed by no less a personage than Washington himself, leading republicans saw in it the final affirmation of the fundamentally corrupting influence of a professional military. Even Alexander Hamilton (who had resigned his commission to take a seat in Congress), otherwise in complete sympathy with the officers grievances, was sufficiently alarmed to move to disband the continental regiments and disperse the troops as rapidly as possible.

With the coming of peace, the small number of regular soldiers--generally of marginal economic and social position--melted into the general population, their crucial contributions largely forgotten. Almost immediately the victories won by these anonymous regulars were obscured by the popular celebration of the "triumph" of the citizen soldiers. The widespread circulation of these myths began to recapture victory in the Revolution for republican ideology.

The Articles of Confederation and The National Security Dilemma:

The signing of the Declaration of Independence caused the 13 former colonies to become 13 independent states. It had been obvious to the leaders of the rebel cause that in order to successfully prosecute resistance to Britain, the states needed to coordinate their efforts and share resources. This had been the primary motivation for forming the original Continental Congress. In late 1776, following the Declaration of Independence, the Congressional delegates wrote and signed the Articles of Confederation. The basic principle of the Articles was that each state would remain "sovereign." No effort was made to define the precise meaning of that term. In time it was generally used by the states as authority to ignore those resolutions of the Continental Congress with which they disagreed.

On numerous occasions during the war the weakness of the Continental Congress nearly resulted in catastrophe for the cause of independence. Congress found itself trapped in an inflationary spiral that caused continental currency to be devalued as rapidly as they printed it. By 1781, a continental pound was worth only about one cent in "hard" money (specie).[15] The states ignored appeals from Congress for arms, supplies, and men with which to support the Army. Most dangerous for the long term viability of the Republic, the states recognized no obligation to settle the debts incurred by the Congress.

18

The perpetual bankruptcy of the central government had been a principal cause of frustration that led to the Newburgh Conspiracy. It also meant that after the war the heavily devalued continental currency became effectively worthless. With the Army disbanded, and the unifying threat of the common British enemy eliminated, the Congress had nothing with which to back-up, or enforce it's resolutions save the willingness of the states to comply. Events demonstrated that the states obeyed or not as they considered it expeditious.[16]

The inherent weakness of the central government under the Articles of Confederation was particularly alarming in light of the many threats and dangers which still confronted the fledgling United States. Although the treaties ending the Revolution called for Britain to evacuate the forts they occupied along the Northwestern Frontier, British garrisons remained present in them. Furthermore, the Indian nations allied to the British during the war remained hostile. The United States also contended with the growing animosity of the Spanish colonies to the South, a disputed border with Canada and the Indian nations, and a rapidly deteriorating relationship with their recent French allies.

Domestic problems dwarfed those of foreign policy. The settlers along the Western frontiers behaved with nearly complete indifference to the laws of the Congress or the states of which they were nominally a part. Their land encroachments acted to exacerbate the relationship with the independent Indian nations as well as to spark rebellions and uprisings of the domestic tribes within the U.S. borders. They frequently occupied tracts of western land (speculation in which formed the backbone of many public treasuries, as well as private fortunes) without regard to legal title. The rural farmers and tradesmen, increasingly impoverished by heavy tax burdens and spiraling inflation, grew contemptuous of their obligations under the tax and tariff laws and began to regard their commerce as a strictly private affair. Collectively, these problems created a situation of near economic anarchy and spawned a growing number of civil disorders. These disorders reached a crescendo in the events of "Shays Rebellion" in Massachusetts in 1786.

Shays Rebellion resulted from the Massachusetts Legislature increasing taxes to defray the enormous debt incurred by the State during the Revolution. The rural westerners, desperately short of the resources necessary to meet these new burdens, began a series of uncoordinated disturbances which quickly coalesced into an armed rebellion led by a noted figure of the Revolution; Daniel Shays. Massachusetts immediate reaction to this rebellion was to call out the local western militia. State authorities were stunned when these units either failed to respond, or mustered only to join the rebels.[17]

Although the rebellion was eventually put down by loyal eastern units, it left many republicans' faith in militia badly shaken, and triggered a wave of anxiety which expanded throughout the country. It also demonstrated to nationally minded men that the unresolved issues of union had now reached a crisis point. This growing crisis resulted in the convening of the Constitutional Convention in May 1787, and the events of Shays Rebellion were never far from the thoughts of the convention delegates during their deliberations.[18] In the wake of these military challenges, a central issue for the nationalists or "federalists" was the question of a national army.

The Federalist Agenda and the Republican Counter Arguments:

The key Federalist figures in the formation of the Constitutional Convention were Washington, Hamilton, and James Madison. Washington and Hamilton's wartime experience convinced them of the need for a standing, disciplined force responsive to the direction of a strong central government. Madison, however, had seen no active military service, and while he was a man of unquestioned brilliance, he was also possessed of deep intellectual contradictions. He came to the nationalist camp reluctantly, but the chaos of the mid-1780s finally persuaded him of the necessity for a strong national authority. He was never comfortable with the concept of a large standing federal army, however, and the force of his arguments did much to mitigate the scope of the federalist military proposals.[19]

In any event, Washington and Hamilton were realists enough to recognize that, ideological objection aside, the state of American finances would render a large standing army beyond the means of the government for a long time to come. Instead they concentrated on measures that would establish strong federal control over the militia, and provisions that would allow the rapid expansion of the small peacetime force in during a major conflict..

The orthodox republicans considered such measures political heresy, and they opposed the military clauses of the Constitution vigorously at every turn. Espousing the tried and true formulas of traditional Enlightenment philosophy, they continued to insist upon the basic soundness of the traditional militia system.[20] Convinced that the militia had brought eventual victory on the battlefield, they used the examples of the abortive conspiracy at Newburgh, and the formation of the Society of the Cincinnati by leading continental officers, to attack what they regarded as the tyrannical designs and neo-aristocratic ambitions of the federalists.

Adding plausibility to the republican arguments was the fact that an overwhelming majority of the nationalists were veterans of the Continental Army, whereas republicans were primarily veterans of the militia.[21] Republicans maintained that the danger posed by a

21

professional army, of any size, far outweighed the dangers bred of civil disorder, invasion, or divided military counsel. Many republicans also feared that a standing army would be used by the executive to illegally support the western settlers against the Indians in the chronic western territorial disputes.

The Standing Army Compromises and the Evolution of the Legion:

The final draft of the Constitution abandoned any attempt to impose meaningful Federal authority over the militia in peacetime, but did, however grudgingly, make allowance for a regular force to garrison the frontier and respond to immediate national emergencies. In 1789, while Congressional debate on a standing force was bogged down amid parliamentary maneuvering, and republican evasiveness, fewer than 600 poorly trained and badly equipped soldiers were enlisted and on duty in the west.[22]

Despite the new authority of the central government, federal finances had yet to be put on a sound footing. Payment of troops in the frontier garrisons continued to be erratic, and provisions and equipment were sometimes scandalously substandard. In 1790, a force of 300 of these regulars, under the command of Brigadier General Josiah Harmar, and backed by 1,300 western militia, conducted a punitive expedition against the Shawnee and allied Indians in response to long standing conflicts between the Indians and settlers in the Ohio and Kentucky territories. This operation accomplished its limited military objective, but failed to achieve the desired political goal of pacifying the Indians. Instead it inflamed the Indians into extending the length and frequency of their raids, and inspired other Indian tribes to open hostilities.[23] Furthermore, controversy over the high number of casualties, and open quarrels between regulars and militia tended to obscure even the modest success' of the operation.

In 1791, Brigadier General Arthur St. Clair, Governor of the Ohio Territory, attempted to conduct another punitive expedition deep into Indian territory. St. Clair took an even larger force of regulars and militia, as well as an artillery train. The quarrels between regulars and militia were even worse on this expedition than on the previous one, however, and St. Clair proved to be an inept and grossly overconfident Indian fighter. In the worst single defeat ever suffered by the US Army, St. Clair's force was ambushed in their poorly sited, and unfortified camp. Over one-half of St. Clair's men were killed in the melee with a strong and well led force of Shawnee and Delaware warriors. The survivors streamed back along the route of advance under no military control, and having abandoned all their equipment.

These two defeats of the fledgling American Army had nearly fatal effects for the young nation. Many western settlers took the defeat of St. Clair's command to signal the final failure of the Federal Government to deal effectively with the Indian problem. This led indirectly to the growing refusal of westerners to comply with federal law. Recognizing the sensitivity of the situation, President Washington won congressional authority to expand the regular establishment to 5,000 men, organize it into a combined force of infantry, artillery, and cavalry known as a Legion, and appoint "Mad" Anthony Wayne as its Major General.

Wayne personally supervised the enlistment, equipping, and training of this force and refused to be rushed into field operations until he was confident it had reached an acceptable level of professionalism. The bleak events in the west also led to renewed congressional interest in the old federalist proposals to restructure the various state militias along uniform lines under federal supervision. The meat of the federalist reforms were written out of the final version, but the legislation (which became the Militia Act of

23

1792) was nonetheless significant in that it set the basic relationship between the Militia and the Regular Army for more than 100 years.

During the period that Wayne was organizing the Legion, the alienation between the western settlers and the Federal Government was growing more acute. This animosity came to a head over the issue of federal tariffs on distilled liquors in the incident known as the Whisky Rebellion. Western distillers refused to pay the tariffs and armed themselves to resist any federal attempt to force the issue. To cope with this situation, Washington called militia from several states to federal service, and prepared to march against the Whisky Rebels.

Before Washington's forces could depart their training camps, however, Wayne's Legion handed the Indians a crushing defeat at the battle of Fallen Timbers, effectively ending the Indian problem in Ohio and Kentucky. When news of this victory, along with President Washington's military preparations, reached the rebels their insurrection quickly collapsed. The operations of the Legion set the basic pattern for the role of regular American forces until the Second World War.

The success of the Legion, combined with the alarm generated by the western uprisings, made it possible for federalists to fight off republican attempts to disband the Legion immediately after a peace treaty had been signed with the Shawnee. In the light of the numerous conflicts endured by the United States in this short period, it seems incredible that any political faction could have still considered disarming the Federal Government. In order to fully understand how such dogmatic political positions could be held by otherwise reasonable men, it will first be necessary to explore the federalist's and republican's common philosophical heritage in detail. Chapter three will trace the foundations of eighteenth century American liberal thought, and how the experiences of the Revolution caused a schism to develop within American political philosophy.

CHAPTER 3

THE ORIGINS OF AMERICAN LIBERALISM

"An armed, disciplined body is, in its essence, dangerous to liberty--undisciplined, it is ruinous to society."[1] This quote by 18th century British statesman Edmund Burke neatly frames the debate and sums up the dilemma faced by the nationalists and republicans during the first decades of the American Republic. In order to fully understand the experiences and ideological schisms that created these two political factions, it is necessary to first examine their common philosophical origins.

One standard American dictionary defines a "Whig" as: "a supporter of the war against England during the American Revolution."[2] By this definition the revolutionary leadership can all be considered to have been Whigs. It is certainly safe to say that, at least until the emergence of recognizable political parties about 1790, they considered themselves to be such. What then did it mean to be a Whig?

More than anything else, to be a Whig meant to be an adherent to the political philosophies of the liberal British thinkers of the eighteenth century, such as John Trenchard, Algernon Sidney, and most seminally, John Locke. Locke's <u>Treatises on Civil Government</u> (1689) was the first coherent exposition of the concept of constitutional democracy.[3] This work set forth the basic principles upon which all later Enlightenment philosophies were to build: the "natural" rights of man, rejection of the "divine" right of Kings, rule by the consent of the people, and a bellicose reappraisal of the "social contract" first posited by Thomas Hobbes:

> . . . Whenever the legislatures endeavor to take away and destroy the property of the people, or to reduce them to slavery under arbitrary power, they put themselves into a state of war with the people, who are thereupon absolved from any further obedience, and are left to the common refuge which God hath provided for all men against force and violence.[4]

So widely read and accepted were Locke's ideas in the American Colonies, that Thomas Jefferson could speak for the entire Continental Congress when he held them to be "self-evident truths" in the Declaration of Independence. Jefferson then proceeded to enumerate the history of George III and Parliament's crimes against the American people, their sovereign property, and their virtuous forbearance: "The history of the present King of Great Britain is a history of repeated injuries and usurpations all having in direct object the establishment of an absolute Tyranny over these states."[5] That Jefferson chose to state the case for independence by framing it in an historical context was no mere literary device. By reviewing the history of the American dispute with Great Britain, Jefferson was appealing to the other consuming intellectual study of colonial Whigs: history.

It is important to note that for an educated American Colonist, the study of history was by no means the casual exercise that it has become for most modern Americans. Men like John Adams, his cousin Sam Adams, James Madison, Richard Henry Lee, and other leading figures of the day read history avidly and deeply, searching it for clues to assist them in navigating the perilous course to resolving their collective disputes with Great Britain. To be educated in that time was to read, and most of what was read was history, or commentary upon history.

Historian Trevor Colbourn made a detailed survey of the titles listed in surviving inventories of colonial public and private libraries, and has found them to be composed overwhelmingly of historical volumes.[6] Colbourn points out that for a back water agricultural society, the Colonies had: "remarkably bookish (if not literary) tastes."[7] And the vast preponderance of English historical writers of the Eighteenth century were men and women of unmistakably liberal leanings.[8]

Fired with the intellectual fervor of the "age of reason," they sought to discern in the panorama of history the keys which would enable them to identify the underlying patterns controlling it. Just as Newton identified and described the universal laws of physics, historians sought the universal laws of history. Furthermore, the category of history itself was more flexible in those times. Much of what we today would consider philosophy, or political science, was then loosely cataloged as history.[9] The term political science, itself coined in the eighteenth century, provides insight into the quest to apply rational, "scientific" methodology to the understanding of social and historical phenomena. For these eighteenth century students, well schooled in Aristotle, the logical place to begin a deliberate study of history was at its beginnings.

H.G. Wells is said to have once remarked that Plutarch is what kept the United States a republic.[10] True or not, the direct influence of classical history on American political thought was significant. A grounding in the classics formed the basis of almost all formal eighteenth century education--hence a "classical education." A person's inability to read Plutarch in the original, however, need have been no barrier. Colbourn's title lists make clear that English translations of Plato, Thucydides, Tacitus, Cicero, Livy, and other ancients were both numerous and popular.

The lessons of Ancient history took on considerable significance when one considers that for eighteenth century men committed to republican ideals, history then offered few contemporary examples of republican government. Except for Revolutionary England under the brief Parliamentary rule, or the experiences of the Netherlands, Venice, or the Swiss Cantons which, arguably, were more oligarchical than republican, the only true democracies had existed in ancient times. Therefore the experiences of the Greek City States and Rome held real and immediate significance for American thinkers.

Viewed through the prism of Whig liberal ideology, these examples offered clear and compelling lessons. Widely popular general works, such as Charles Rollin's Ancient History, offered an abridged version of the classics using carefully selected passages that the author considered to be: "most useful and entertaining . . . most instructive."[11] That these passages tended to depict a brave, noble and free Athens destroyed by its own immoderate indulgence, and the venality of a Pericles corrupted by power and ambition, speaks eloquently about what Rollins considered to be most instructive.

To the Whig historians, the experience of the Roman Republic was also particularly illuminating. The Rise of Rome to world domination was attributed to the commendable civic and moral virtues of her free citizens. It was the free militia of Rome that had made her a great Empire -- its lapse into degeneracy and decadence that had brought the Empire low: "A luxurious people were disinclined to do their own fighting, and by hiring others to do it for them they invited tyranny and military despotism."[12] In the Whig Historiography a major turning point for the republic came when the Ancient militia system was superseded by a professional standing army.

A standing army was an open invitation to abuse, and Whig historians were quick to note that tyranny, in the guise of Julius Ceaser, was not long in seizing upon the Army as an instrument to enslave the people. In the works of Charles Rollin, Oliver Goldsmith, and the other "enlightened" commentators, Ceaser was the archetypical tyrant. Having seized power on the pretext of protecting the state, he was the embodiment of corrupt power and unbridled ambition. A professional soldier leading professional (read mercenary) soldiers, Ceaser conquered the champions of the free Senate with the intention of subordinating Rome to his will.

The Roman senatorial conspirators, Cassius, Cato, and Brutus, were invariably presented as the heroes of the episode, bravely--if futilely--standing forth to strike down the enemy of liberty in order to defend the people's rights.[13] The largely sympathetic treatment accorded Ceaser in modern American popular mythology was conspicuously absent in the colonial period.[14] That the conspirators failed was viewed not as an invalidation of republican ideals, but as an indictment of the decadence of the Roman people: "[Rome rose] by temperance . . . and fell by luxury."[15] Colbourn's survey of the historical literature of the period demonstrates that, for the Whig historians, the unmistakable engine of the Roman Republic's destruction was a standing army: ". . . standing armies enslaved that great people, and their excellent militia and freedom perished together."[16]

The study of Ancient history created a common frame of reference, underpinning the work of Whig writers on both sides of the Atlantic. Englishman John Trenchard adopted the nom-de-plume "Cato" for his scathing pamphlet attacks on the regular army in Britain in the

30

1730's, confident that the name alone would vividly indicate his point of view.[17] John Jay, James Madison, and Alexander Hamilton likewise published their defense of the proposed Constitution over the collective signature "Publius" clearly having intended to invoke the spirit of the early Roman republic.[18] The pseudonyms chosen by others were equally evocative; Alexander Hanson--Aristides, David Ramsay--Civus, John Dickinson--Fabius, James Iredel--Marcus.[19] As influential as these Ancient works were, however, the real historical case for Whig ideology was to be made through a close analysis of British history since the Tudor monarchs. In the words of John Jay:

> The history of Great Britain is the one with which we are in general best acquainted, and it gives us many useful lessons. We may profit by their experience without paying the price which it cost them.[20]

The political History of Great Britain was, in the broad strokes of the Whig historian, a history of the struggle of the people, as represented by Parliament, to secure their rights against the prerogatives of the Crown (to include a large proportion of the Peerage). The roots of this struggle go back at least to the Norman conquest of Saxon England, and, indeed, the Whig literature of the period is replete with approving mention of the mythic Saxon militia and appeals to the simple Saxon "virtues" of ancient times.[21]

With the dawn of the Renaissance at the end the Hundred years War, the ancient feudal levy system collapsed, and warfare was dominated by hired professional mercenaries loyal to whoever could pay them. The Tudor monarchs consolidated their power over Britain with the use of just such mercenary troops and used them to intimidate, or eliminate potential internal of external resistance.[22] Thereafter, a dominant concern for British monarchs jealous of their prerogatives

31

would be the circular requirements to secure more revenue to pay for troops, by hiring more troops to enforce their access to revenue.

This development coincided with the rise of a powerful middle class grown wealthy by the newly expanding mercantile opportunities in overseas trade. The revival of learning which gave the Renaissance its name, had a tremendous impact on this increasingly literate middle class. The rediscovered interest in the ancient philosophers led a growing body of men to question the authority of the Roman Church, and the absolute right of kings. In time, the merchant class began to agitate for its own interests, and in those struggles were born the Protestant objections to the traditional authority of the Catholic Church which led to the Reformation. For the next 150 years the political conflicts of Britain and Europe were overlaid with an element of religious fanaticism which frequently animated both Catholics and Protestants to acts of irrational savagery.

In England, the Protestant churches, overwhelmingly composed of commoners initially, developed an abiding mistrust of Royal authority as a result of the repeated repressions inflicted upon them by reactionary Catholic monarchs such as "Bloody" Mary and James II. This period saw the birth of the Puritan sects whose eventual immigration to North America in order to escape religious persecution gave their experience particular significance to their colonial descendants. For the Whig historian, however, the seminal episode in English history was the great drama played out between Parliament and the Crown between 1640 and 1689 known as the English Civil Wars.

The second of the Stuart monarchs, Charles I of England, was a devotee of the concept of the "divine right of kings." In Charles' eyes, the king was above the common law. Louis XIV's statement of some years later, "I am the state," neatly summed up Charles' attitude towards royal prerogative.[23] Charles' arrogance ensured that he quarreled constantly with Parliament, and his obvious preference for a "High" Church of England, controlled by Bishops and a traditional clerical hierarchy, aroused the particular antipathy of the Scottish Presbyterians, Lutherans, and other puritan sects.

These disputes led to perennial struggles between Charles and Parliament over money. Between 1625 and 1640, Charles dissolved Parliament three times for refusing to grant him revenues. The continued financial strain of Charles' conflicts with the Scots, however, forced him to recall Parliament in 1640 to seek new money for his armies. The new Parliament immediately passed the Triennial Act, requiring the King to summon Parliament every three years, dissolved the Star Chamber and High Commission (bodies by which Charles had circumvented the authority of Parliament), and submitted the Nineteen Propositions (reforms) codifying the relationship between Parliament and Monarch.

Frustrated, Charles attempted to arrest five leading members of Parliament, and tried to impose taxes without Parliamentary approval. In response Parliament raised an army of resistance and open civil war raged until 1645 when Charles was finally defeated by Oliver Cromwell's New Model Army at the Battle of Naseby. The following year, Charles surrendered to the Scots who, in turn, surrendered him to Parliament in 1647. In 1649, at the instigation of the Army, Charles was tried for treason and executed, after which England was governed as a republic until 1660.

Over the course of these conflicts the parliamentary army, first under Lord Fairfax, and then Cromwell, came to increasingly dominate Parliamentary affairs. The "New Model" Army, raised in 1544 by Fairfax, with significant assistance from Cromwell, was in every sense a modern standing army. The soldiers were thoroughly disciplined, professionally trained, and organized on a standard pattern. The officers were chosen for their reliability and competence, and owed their allegiance to their Commanders.[24]

Charles' son, Charles II, became King following his father's death. Over the next 12 years he made repeated attempts to restore the Stuart throne in England. In the process of countering these challenges, and coping with numerous other military conflicts as Lieutenant General of the Army, Cromwell established himself as the effective military dictator of England. In 1653, Cromwell eliminated the last vestiges of resistance to his authority by dissolving Parliament and declaring himself "Lord Protector" of England. Cromwell died in power in 1658, and was succeeded as Protector by his son Richard.

Richard, never popular, and demonstrably lacking in the skills of his father, was deposed by the Army after a brief reign, and the governance of England was restored to Parliamentary authority. In 1660, in an effort to forestall the possibility of a new dictator, a Parliamentary convention restored Charles II to the throne of England. A majority in Parliament believed that restoring the traditional Crown, albeit with greatly circumscribed powers, was safer than risking the probability of a renewed military dictatorship.

Almost immediately Charles II began to machinate against the restrictions imposed upon him by the Convention Parliament. In 1661 Charles managed to seat a Parliament largely favorable to his designs, and was thereby able to secure the passage of a series of repressive laws. Though nominally a Protestant, Charles retained strong Catholic sympathies. During his exiles in France he had become close with the Catholic monarch Louis XIV. In 1670 Charles signed a secret treaty with Louis to restore Roman Catholicism to England. It remains unclear, however, whether he was seriously committed to this goal, or if this was just a gesture to ensure the continued financial support

34

from Louis that enabled him to maintain a sumptuous court life despite a stingy Parliament.[25]   In 1673, despite the King's vigorous attempts to prevent it, a wary Parliament passed the "Test Act" designed to ban Roman Catholics from holding Public Office.   Charles was furious at the imposition of yet another legal impediment to his goal of restoring, and possibly even expanding the lost prerogatives of his father.

In 1679, a then fully aroused Parliament passed the Act of Habeas Corpus which forbade imprisonment without trial.   Charles, however, managed to frustrate Parliament's attempt to pass the Bill of Exclusion which would have blocked Charles' Catholic brother, the Duke of York from succeeding to the throne.   Charles dismissed the sitting Parliament, and then rejected a series of petitions calling for a new one.   For obscure reasons, these petitioners became known as Whigs and the royalist supporters as Tories.

Upon the Death of Charles II in 1685, Catholic James II ascended to the throne.   In 1686, James disregarded the Test Act and appointed Roman Catholics to high offices.   To thwart his Anglican opposition the following year, he issued the "Declaration of Liberty of Conscience" which extended legal toleration to all religions. This move was viewed by the Protestant majority as a cynical attempt to cloak a Catholic conspiracy in the guise of liberal philanthropy.   The action was especially alarming in view of the close ties between the Stuarts and Louis the XIV, who, in 1685, had banned all religions except Roman Catholicism in France.

In 1688, Parliament rose against James in the event known to Whig historians as the "Glorious Revolution."   Parliament invited Protestant William III of the Netherlands (the husband of Mary Stuart, an heir to the thrown) to "save" England from Roman Catholicism. William landed in Britain with a small force and after a brief struggle, James II fled to permanent exile in France. In 1689 the Convention Parliament issued the "Bill of Rights", explicitly delineating the rights of free Englishmen and converting Great Britain into a constitutional monarchy.

Over the course of those Fifty tumultuous years were solidified all of the themes which defined 18th century liberal political thought; the corrosive effect of decadence on the virtue of a free people, the inherent perfidity of hereditary monarchy, the corruptive influence of centralized power, and the constant danger posed by standing armies to the rights and liberties of a free citizenry. Whig historiographical accounts of these events filled the book cases of educated colonial Americans.

The works of liberal historians such as Gilbert Burnet, Edmund Ludlow, Paul Rapin, David Hume, Catherine Macaulay, and Lord Clarendon were all available in multiple editions.[26] The Political-Historical commentaries of Lord Bolingbroke, John Trenchard, Joseph Chamberlain, Charles Montesquieu, and Algernon Sidney were all in constant demand, and figured prominently in the bookseller's advertisements.[27]

While reinforcing their conviction in the justice of their claim to the basic rights of Englishmen, the Whig interpretations simultaneously fostered in the American colonial mind that suspicion of authority, and ready belief in royal conspiracy, which would translate petition to rebellion, and rebellion to revolution. The examples, from Pericles to Cromwell, of centralized power grown corrupt, also convinced many of the menace of powerful central government. Of particular interest to these were the memoirs of Edmund Ludlow. Ludlow, a member of the Parliament which voted to execute Charles I, became an embittered critic of Cromwell and left this warning: "men may learn from the issue of the Cromwellian tyranny, that liberty and a standing army are incompatible."[28]

These then were the common intellectual precepts shared by American radicals on the eve of the Revolution; an abiding belief in the singular virtue of the American "race", apprehension of the possibility of a Royal/Parliamentary conspiracy against the colonials' rights as Englishmen, an almost paranoid obsession with the nefarious influence of a standing army, and a nearly religious faith in militia as the one true safe-guard of the people's liberty, and as a true reflection of their civic virtue.

"In free countries, as people work for themselves, so they fight for for themselves; But in arbitrary countries, it is all the same to the people, in point of interest, who conquers them."[29] This statement by John Trenchard neatly summed up the conviction held by most American Whigs that aside from practical or economic considerations, American reliance on militia for the defense of the Colonies was proof that they were indeed a virtuous society worthy of the Freedom they sought.

The military events of the first year of rebellion seemed to confirm the radicals faith in militia. At Lexington and Concord the embattled farmers gave a good account of themselves. Fired by the "Rage Militaire", militia units mustered rapidly around the heights of Boston, and threw up earth work defenses with a speed and skill that astonished the British professionals.[30] After the spirited defense of Breed's Hill, and the subsequent evacuation of the British forces to Nova Scotia, confidence ran high among rebel leaders that the "peculiar genius" of the American people was more than a match for British professionalism. Sam Adams said that the militia had: "behaved with an Intrepidity becoming those who fight for their liberties against the

37

mercenary soldiers of a Tyrant."[31] Thomas Jefferson's confidence moved him to write a friend: "want of discipline [could be overcome] by native courage and . . . animation in the cause."[32]

The newly appointed commander, George Washington, though, had a very different reaction after surveying the American siege lines in June 1775. An inherently conservative military thinker, Washington appalled at the indiscipline of the militia units, and was alarmed by the filth and disorder of their camps.[33] With the willing assistance of Major General Charles Lee, late of His Majesty's Service, but now an enthusiastic supporter of the rebellion, and Horatio Gates, also an experienced soldier, Washington managed to impose a degree of discipline on the chaos in a remarkably short time.

Washington's first concern was to weed out of the Army's Officer Corps the derelict, incompetent, and the grossly intemperant. The majority of the officers had been elected by their companies or regiments and their commitment to imposing military discipline on their constituency was minimal. There were also many state officers appointed because of their political or family influence who possessed neither the character, nor ability to lead soldiers on active service. Although Washington's authority over the various militia units was vague, within the first month he had, by one stratagem or another, transferred, discharged, or court marshaled dozens of the worst cases, and the others were beginning to come around.[34]

Washington also effected a thorough reorganization of his forces. The militia units around Boston were enlisted (with the wary consent of their colonies) into the "Continental" service to the end of the year. Regiments were grouped into brigades, and the brigades apportioned to manageable sections of the lines. Washington formed the more talented young officers into the beginnings of a coherent staff, and soon they began to make progress in taming the chaotic supply arrangements. By the end of July, a comparative degree of order had been achieved in the lines, and Washington began to feel a small confidence that the situation was coming into hand.[35]

Remarkably, even this modicum of military regularity was cause for uneasiness among some of the more ardent Whig ideologists. Leading Massachusetts statesman Elbridge Gerry approved of Washington's attempts to bring order to the camps, but objected to relinquishing full control of state troops and wanted the Legislature to determine the number of troops detailed to specific tasks, and their length of duty, even when called to service within their home colony.

As early as mid-summer 1775, fellow legislator, Sam Adams was calling the army around Boston, "a standing army," and began criticizing Washington's establishment of a central Continental headquarters whose authority over the general militia superseded that of provincial officers.[36] Even John Adams, who had done more than any other individual to promote Washington's appointment, was beginning to have twinges of concern about placing so much potential power in the hands of one man, and he resolved to be a "strict spy" and to keep the affairs of the Continental Commander under meticulous "servileness."[37]

1776 was the major turning point for American revolutionary military policy. The army which Washington and his officers had so laboriously organized around Boston evaporated at the end of their short enlistments in December 1775. Congress asked the various colonies (states after July 1776) to furnish short enlistment regiments to replace those mustering out. To reinforce these, local militia units were rotated every month or so to allow the men to do necessary work at home. By the spring of '76, however, the "Rage Militaire" had subsided, and to fill their quotas for Continental volunteers, many communities sent the sweepings of their jails and public houses.

While attempting to convert this ragged assemblage into effective brigades, Washington was driven to distraction by the capricious comings and goings of the general militia bands. Since the general militia units were effectively beyond the continental officers ability to control, their principle effect in camp was to destroy what modicum of discipline had been successfully translated to the one year volunteers.[38] With this material, the Continental Commander was attempting to prepare for the expected return of the British main Force, as well as direct operations in Canada.

When the British finally did strike back in the late spring, the almost unbroken string of staggering defeats and humiliations experienced by Washington's forces as they retreated from Canada, New York, and across New Jersey, caused a crisis of confidence in the policy of reliance on the civic motivation of patriotic citizens. Much of the defeat in New York could be attributed to the inexperience of American commanders, and the limited experience and poor engineering skills of novice American staff officers. It could not be denied, however, that on more than one occasion rebel troops had simply panicked in the face of British forces greatly inferior in number. On August 25, John Adams confided to a friend: "I fear that human nature will be found to be the same in America as it has been in Europe, and that the true principle of liberty will not be attended to."[39]

Washington was driven near despair by his inability to effect meaningful reform on his Army. He shared his bitter frustration in a letter to his cousin Lund Washington:

> I see the impossibility of serving with reputation, or doing any essential service for the cause by continuing in command, and yet I am told that if I quit the command, inevitable ruin will follow from the distraction that will ensue. . . . I am fully persuaded that under such a system as has been adopted, [Short term

enlistments and reliance on general militia] I cannot have the least chance for reputation, nor those allowances [for his failures] made which the nature of the case requires. . . .[40]

Washington wanted a greatly expanded Continental Army composed of long term (3 years minimum) volunteers, raised in the respective states, but under the exclusive operational control of the Continental military authorities. He also wanted a reformed system of officer acquisition and promotion. Washington sought control of all officer appointments, and wished to base promotions on the recommendation of a properly constituted board of officers who would then submit lists of names for final approval by Congress. Finally he wanted permission to offer substantial "bounties" as an inducement to enlistment, and to set military wages at a level competitive with those of common farm laborers, or other low skilled occupations in order to attract better recruits, and to ease the sting of the harsh discipline he intended to impose.[41] Beginning in early July 1776, Washington and several other respected continental officers began, with increasing urgency, to press Congress to enact these measures.

The passage of the Declaration of Independence greatly raised the stakes of the war for the leaders of the rebellion. Success could no longer be measured by forcing a receptive hearing in Parliament. Once the break with Great Britain was irrevocable, the Whig leaders only hope to secure an independent nation (not to mention avoiding a hangman's noose) lay in battlefield victory. To many Whig ideologs, however, the means of that victory were at least as important as the victory itself. If victory were secured only by recourse to the establishment of hated regular soldiers, what would that say about the new race of men who's virtues Benjamin Franklin and Thomas Jefferson were extolling? It was with considerable trepidation that congressional legislators took the first halting steps toward an army based on the traditional European model.

Predictably, Congress did not give Washington everything he asked for. Because of the stark necessity to take some kind of action or face imminent defeat, and not without much debate and objection, Congress finally voted to approve the three year enlistments. Authority to appoint officers and apportion of promotions, however, remained with the state authorities. Furthermore, quotas for raising the regiments of "Continental Line" were assigned to the various states without any mechanism to ensure they would be fulfilled. This shortcoming was to plague Washington for the remainder of the war. Washington undoubtably spoke for the majority of continental officers by seeking a more "regular" establishment. There was, however, one powerful and respected military voice counseling a separate course.

Charles Lee was the most experienced soldier in the Continental Army. He had risen to the rank of Lieutenant Colonel in the regular British Army and had held a posting as a Major General in the service of the King of Poland. He had seen action in North America during the Seven Years War, as well as participating in campaigns in Portugal, Hungary and the Balkans. He was well mannered, well read, charming, and one of the great eccentrics in American History.

He shared (or at least professed to share) the same commitment to Whig ideologies possessed by the leading men of the Continental Congress, and could speak knowledgeably with them about any related subject. He greatly impressed John Adams (no easy trick) and others, and they arranged to appoint him to the highest position politically practical, 2nd Major General (3rd in Command) of the Continental forces at Boston. Significantly, for an officer of his times and background, he had a remarkable amount of experience in irregular warfare, and was fully committed to the policy of reliance upon militia as had been originally posited by the colonial liberal intelligentsia.[42]

Lee seems to have believed (with some reason) that his appointment under Washington was a political expedient, and that it was Congress' intention that he would mentor and guide Washington through all significant military decisions. As it became clear to him that Washington had very firm military opinions of his own, however, Lee grew disaffected with his Commander. Lee believed that Washington's attempts to meet the British regulars in conventional style was an invitation to disaster. He favored a strategy of small unit hit and run operations (what today would be considered guerrilla tactics) that would erode British strength, while minimizing the risks to American forces.

When it became clear that the Commander-in-Chief had no intention of adopting these tactics wholesale, Lee began a prodigious correspondence with various influential members of Congress who were themselves highly critical of Washington's leadership. Apparently, the object of this correspondence was to erode Congressional confidence in Washington's military abilities. The details of this episode, known as the "Conway Cabal," remain a matter of historical debate and speculation. From the extant documents and his later actions it seems clear that Lee was agitating with the goal of having Washington removed, and himself given supreme command. Whether or not these machinations were ever part of a coherent plot involving other figures with the same goals, however, remains unresolved.[43] The issue became moot after Lee was captured by a British patrol in December 1776.

For the issue of American defense policy--if not for Washington personally--the question of a conspiracy was not as important as the message being sent to the congressional republican ideologs. In the

43

professional opinion of a most respected senior officer, the militia was functioning as theory indicated it should. Armed with Lee's opinion, unshakable republicans could argue that, had Congress not been panicked by the force of conservative argument into prematurely abandoning the militia policy, the system would have vindicated itself. Washington would not have endorsed that sentiment, but he did not advocate an unequivocal rejection of the militia concept. Rather, he concluded, it was the traditional militia system that was incapable of responding to the crisis of the Revolution.

Don Higgenbotham has argued that during the Revolution, and especially in the Historiography that has grown up since, Washington's views on militia have been greatly distorted. Many contemporaries and later historians drew their conclusions about Washington's sentiments from such definitive statements of his as: "Regular troops are alone equal to the exigencies of modern war, as well for defense as offense, and whenever a substitute is attempted it must prove illusory and ruinous,"[44] and "Short enlistments and a mistaken dependence upon militia, have been the origin of all our misfortunes, ..."[45] and "To place any dependence upon militia is assuredly resting upon a broken staff. . . . ."[46]

Higgenbotham notes, however, that these statements, written during the gloomiest and most desperate periods of the war, tell only part of the story. Washington certainly believed that the militia was capable of performing the basic missions of policing and patrolling the states. He also believed that the general militia was capable of performing most local defense tasks likely to be encountered by the majority of American communities during the war; defending against Indian raids, repulsing enemy patrols, or engaging loyalist militia forces. As Washington wrote to a state governor while refusing a request to detach a large body of continental regulars to be used as garrison troops; "The Militia shall be more than competent to all purposes [of internal security]."[47] It was the militia's failures in the major battles that led Washington to doubt their effectiveness in open warfare against a well disciplined regular force.

Higgenbotham hypothesizes that: "In Washington's view, the Continentals and militia had separate, although mutually supportive roles to play."[48] He views the Washington strategy as one of keeping the regular establishment together both as a force capable of standing up to British professionalism in the open field, and as a symbol of the states' unity of purpose and resolve. Wahington believed this force must not be fettered away piecemeal by detaching regiments across the breadth of the country to provide routine security. That mission was the proper province of the local militia.

Washington's recorded sentiments later in the War, and throughout his remaining public career, support this assessment. Washington would remain a strong advocate of militia reform during his life, but he never, save for those dark, desperate periods in 1776 and 1780, advocated the system be abandoned and replaced by a exclusively regular establishment.[49] The economics of the issue undoubtedly played some role in his assessment, but it is also obvious from his actions and remarks to the assembled officers at the Newburgh confrontation that he remained loyal to the basic tenants of his Whig ideology even after the trials and disillusionments of the war.

In his study of Republican theory and practice during the Revolution, John Todd White argues that: "As civilians began to lose faith in American virtue, they began to look upon the Continental Army as little different from the standing armies of Europe."[50] He asserts that: "Army officers in particular began to be viewed as a source of the corruption of American republicanism."[51] White believes it was in reaction to this public hostility that the officer corps developed its animosity to the Congress and created the civil-military rift so evident at the end of the War.

While this argument undoubtedly contains some truth, it seems improbable that men who were commonly viewed as dangerous and corrupt, would have moved so easily and so frequently among civilian positions of respect and elective office.[52] Certainly the almost universal reverence held for George Washington by a people so sensitive of their personal liberties, tends not to support the contention that he was viewed as presiding over a band of would-be autocrats.

Possibly, White has missed something a good bit more basic, and more universal in soldiering. This is what Bill Mauldin described as "the brotherhood of them what's been shot at."[53] The initial hostility felt by the Continental Army officers was more likely of the variety to be found in any group of military men, sharing a common danger, hardship, and privation while contemplating the, to them, incomprehensible decisions made by well fed politicians hundreds of miles away in a warm, clean room.

The accumulation of frequently criminal negligence and mismanagement exhibited by Congress and the state authorities in failing to properly feed, clothe, equip, or pay the soldiers deepened this completely unexceptional sentiment into something approaching contempt.[54] Men of action, they were not inclined to sympathy for Congress' chronic powerlessness to achieve any significant reform. These officers also viewed with anger and dismay the congressional maneuverings by certain republican legislators designed to bilk them out of the pensions, and other compensations they had been promised during the War.

It was as a result of these struggles over pay and renumeration, far more than any republican concern over "loss of virtue," that caused the Continental Army to be regarded as similar to a European standing army by the general populace. Sensitive republican ideologs were certainly concerned about the prominent role played by regular troops in the American victory. For the mass of the people, however, it was the continental officers social affectations, and the perception of the officers efforts as grasping, and motivated by a desire to line their pockets at the public's expense, that caused the popular backlash of 1783.

Over the course of the War, the continental officers collectively came to regard themselves not as inimicable to the peoples virtue, but as the true repository and reflection of that virtue. The experience of protracted war had not eroded their sense of civic virtue, but rather exaggerated it until they felt a keen moral superiority over their civilian brethren--a sentiment not calculated to endear them to their fellow citizens. These officers' sense of unique sacrifice, superior virtue, and injured pride led them to consider mutiny at the Newburgh encampment in the last months of the War. This "Newburgh Conspiracy" brought into bold relief the split within American Whig ideology that had developed in the course of seven years of war.

The exigencies, military, political, and economic, that proved necessary to translate American independence from ideological theory to practical reality had fundamentally altered the political/philosophical, views held by many of the revolutionary Whigs. A large group of nationalists had formed in the Continental Congress and the Army, began to view a government possessed of strong central powers--a "Federal" system--as the best hope to secure and expand the liberties newly won.

These nationalists--later "federalists," were vigorously opposed by those leaders who remained committed to the original, traditional liberal ideologies. The public and private debates between these factions would dominate American politics until the War of 1812. Their struggles created the compartmented government of divided powers that is the unique American contribution to democratic thought. A critical issue in these debates was the role, composition, and safeguards against the military in a peacetime society. From 1783 to 1800, a passionate national argument raged on the subject of: "how an armed forces necessary for external security could be prevented from crushing internal liberties?"[55]

CHAPTER 4

THE DEBATES 1783 TO 1789

In April of 1783, with the Newburgh crisis safely resolved, a congressional committee chaired by Alexander Hamilton was appointed to make recommendations on a peacetime military establishment for the new nation. Hamilton's first action was to request official recommendations from Secretary at War Benjamin Lincoln, and from the Commander-in-Chief, George Washington. Before replying, Washington solicited the views of trusted senior officers (prominently Steuben, Knox, and Pickering), and from New York Governor George Clinton (since New York's strategic location forced it to bear the brunt of wartime hardships). Integrating these views with his own, Washington submitted his "Sentiments on a Peace Establishment" to Hamilton's committee on 2 May 1783.[1]

Sentiments on a Peace Establishment is among the most important documents in the history of United States defense policy. Combining the views of key officers and officials with over seven years experience of administering, training, and leading both continental and militia soldiers, and with combat experience against both British regulars and Indian hostiles, it represents the mature recommendations of America's most able revolutionary military leaders. While fully mindful of both the state of continental finances, and the ideological prejudices against a regular force, Washington and his colleague were nonetheless unanimous in recommending a small standing army:

> Altho' a large standing Army in time of Peace hath ever been considered dangerous to the liberties of a Country, yet a few Troops, under certain circumstances, are not only safe, but

indispensably necessary. Fortunately for us our relative situation requires but few.[2]

That Washington was keenly aware of the economic burdens posed by a permanent military, and that he was cognizant of the full range of military threats to America, and the limitations of even a large standing force was also apparent:

> But if our danger from those powers was more imminent, yet we are too poor to maintain a standing Army adequate to our defense [from the regular forces of Europe], and was our Country more populous and rich, still it could not be done without great oppression of the people. Besides, as soon as we are able to raise funds more than adequate to the discharge of the Debts incurred by the Revolution, it may become a question worthy of consideration, whether the surplus should not be applied in preparations for building and equiping a Navy, without which we could neither protect our Commerce, nor yield that Assistance to each other, which, on such an extent of Sea-Coast, our mutual Safety would require.[3]

Washington recommended a standing army of 2631 officers and men composing four regiments of infantry and one of artillery. These troops were to be divided among posts along the frontier, and would provide the garrisons for West Point and other national magazines. Their mission would be to police the territories, provide early warning against attack from British Canada, French Louisiana, or Spanish Florida, and most importantly, provide a check against depredations by the Indian Nations along the borders of the U.S.: ". . . It may be policy and oeconomy (sic.), to appear respectable in the eyes of the Indians, at the Commencement of our National Intercourse and Traffic with them."[4]

Vital as these peacetime roles were, Washington viewed the regular establishment's greatest contribution as providing a trained and disciplined body around which the various militia organizations could coalesce, and from which cadre could be selected in time of emergency for the organization of additional regiments. He

deliberately included a compliment of officers greater than that
normally required for a regiment both to provide sufficient officers
for the numerous detached garrisons, and to: " . . . give us a Number
of Officers well skilled in the Theory and Art of War, who will be
ready on any occasion, to mix and diffuse their knowledge of Discipline
to other Corps. . . ."[5]

Washington knew that a force of 2600 men, even concentrated
into a single formation, much less spread along the length of America's
extensive frontiers, was inadequate to resist any significant invasion
force. He therefore recommended that the primary burden for the
defense of the United States remain on the militia. Despite his
frustrating experiences with militia during the war, he recognized
that, for reasons of both economy, and political expediency, reliance
upon militia was the only realistic alternative for the young republic.
As Washington saw it, the task was to centralize and standardize the
militia in order to place it on a footing capable of meeting the actual
military requirements.

In framing this, his most essential defense policy proposal,
Washington intuitively selected arguments most likely to sway the
traditionally republican members of Congress. To demonstrate his
familiarity with the liberal historical tradition, he first reminded
them of the triumphs of the ancient Greek and Roman militias during:
"their most virtuous and Patriotic ages." Washington enumerated the
success' of the centralized Swiss militia in preserving that small
nation's independence despite being surrounded by powerful, autocratic
neighbors.[6] He then recast the traditional Whig militia philosophy in
terms of a legal obligation:

> . . . The only probable means of preventing insult or hostility
> for any length of time . . . is to put the National Militia in
> such a condition as that they may appear truly respectable in the

Eyes of our Friends and formidable to those who would otherwise become our enemies.

. . . It may be laid down as a primary position, and basis of our system that every Citizen who enjoys the protection of a free Government, owes not only a proportion of his property, but even of his personal services to the defense of it, and consequently that the Citizens of America . . . should be borne on the Militia Rolls.[7]

Washington's choice of the terms "National Militia" and "Citizens of America" was careful and deliberate. He was calling for a reorganization of the existing state militia systems into a single centrally established system in which the states would share responsibility for the militia with the national government. In exchange for a generous subsidy to offset the cost of the troops, Washington planned that the state militias adhere to a uniform set of regulations, organizations and equipment. He also advocated a system whereby the militia would be grouped into categories corresponding to age, and that each regiment include, in addition to the normal compliment of battalions and companies, one "light" Company. In Washington's scheme, the light companies would be composed of special volunteers between the ages of 18 and 25 who would receive more intensive training and the best equipment.

These light companies would constitute a trained and disciplined ready reserve immediately available to respond to local or national emergency. Washington recommended that light company officers be appointed by Congress, and that the National Government pay the full expenses of raising and training these organizations in exchange for the right, during national emergency, to use them anywhere without special permission from the state governors or legislatures.

The remainder of Washington's Sentiments concerned itself with the establishment of frontier posts, suggestions for basic regulations, matters of administration to govern the proposed regular forces, and the establishment of a military academy: ". . . calculated to keep

alive and diffuse the knowledge of the Military Art."[8] Under separate
cover, Major General Von Steuben submitted a more detailed plan for a
national military academy, and Secretary at War Benjamin Lincoln
provided detailed recommendations for the establishment and positioning
of five "Magazines" [depots] for the storage of arms, ammunition, and
accouterments. Lincoln also made specific suggestions for the
establishment of native: "military manufactories and elaboratories
[sic]."[9]

        Washington kept the mechanisms by which state compliance with
these provisions would be enforced deliberately vague in his proposal.
With good reason, he must have been afraid of prematurely alienating
the more parochial and reactionary republican delegates. Clearly,
Washington believed and hoped, that the peace establishment would tend
to increase the power of the central government, and promote a sense of
nationalism through service in the unified militia. That these were
important considerations for Washington is made apparent by another
document he penned in June of 1783 known as the "Circular to the
States."

        The Circular to the States was a kind of valedictory Washington
addressed to the governors and legislatures of the various states. In
it, Washington expressed his desire to present his thoughts on the
major is es confronting the new republic prior to his resignation as
Commander-in-Chief.[10] As such, it represents the first comprehensive
expostulation of the new nationalist philosophy that evolved within the
framework of traditional Whig ideology during the course of the
Revolution.

        Washington began by praising the efforts and sacrifices of the
states in the conflict just passed, and then expressed his, "conviction
of the importance of the present crisis," by which he meant the

strained financial, and political circumstances of the Confederation, and the external threats still facing the Nation.[11] He then proceeded to explain the conclusions he had drawn from his reflections on these matters:

> There are four things, which I humbly conceive, are essential to the well being, I may even venture to say, to the existence of the United States as an Independent Power:

> 1st. An indissoluble Union of the States under one Federal Head.

> 2dly. A sacred regard to Public Justice.

> 3dly. The adoption of a proper Peace Establishment, and

> 4thly. The prevalence of that pacific and friendly Disposition, among the People of the United States, which will induce them to forget their local prejudices and policies, to make those mutual concessions which are requisite to the general prosperity, and in some instances, to sacrifice their individual advantages to the interests of the Community.[12]

These four points neatly encapsulate the nationalist position in 1783. The reference to "Public Justice" was a none too subtle reminder of the states' failure to provide funds, or approve mechanisms by which to retire the enormous public war debt incurred by the Continental Congress. Washington's inclusion of this point indicates his conviction that the interests of the individual states were as yet too parochial to effectively discharge the obligations and responsibilities incurred by the Congress on behalf of all. In Washington's estimation, therefore, the central government needed to be made strong enough to overcome these selfish instincts. Washington regarded a centralized military establishment as offering the twin virtues of providing a truly effective defense, and as serving as a catalyst for effecting a closer union among the States.

Eight years of struggle and sacrifice on behalf of the United States as a whole had imparted to Washington and many of his subordinates a sense of national identity that greatly transcended the narrow parochial bonds of their individual states. Washington aimed to see this new national identity imparted to the people at large. The adherents of this new philosophy (primarily Continental Army officers and like minded members of Congress) did not, at least initially, reject the traditional pillars of republican ideology, but rather, viewed their position as modifying republicanism's theoretical constructs to fit the actual findings of revolutionary experiment.[13]

The nationalists concluded that the militia system could work, but not as originally postulated. Certain modifications, such as a centralized system to enforce compliance and impose discipline, needed to be made in order to compensate for weaknesses in the character of individuals. Their experiences convinced them that raw republican fervor was fickle and unreliable, but they believed it could be replaced by a superior patriotism instilled through professional training and discipline. Nationalists held that even if public virtue did not well up as a natural consequence of political freedom, in the way that traditional republican philosophy claimed that it should, at least, a reasonable approximation of such virtue could be instilled through the disciplined discharge of public responsibilities. Washington and his lieutenants saw the peace establishment as an excellent vehicle for the indoctrination of those public virtue

Combining the reports of Washington and Lincoln with other ideas, Hamilton's committee returned a report to Congress in mid June 1783. The Hamilton proposal differed significantly from Washington's. It was considerably less politically subtle than Washington's plan, and was blatantly in-sensitive to the concerns of the republican ideologs. Hamilton's plan also failed to allow for for the inevitable petty local jealousies arising from the complete relinquishment of state militia control.

Hamilton proposed a regular army of over 3000 men composed of soldiers enlisted for terms of six years. Congress would have complete authority over the recruitment of soldiers, appointment of officers, and the provision of arms and equipment. In addition, Hamilton recommended that Congress sponsor an elite corps of volunteers, or "trained bands" within the larger cities. The trained bands were to constitute a Continental Army reserve composed of part-time soldiers willing to enlist for eight year terms. They were to participate in bimonthly training sessions at the company level, and once per month with the entire regiment.[14]

Presumably in an effort to placate the state's anxiety over the presence of national troops in their major cities, Hamilton's plan limited the total number of these volunteers such that they would not exceed two percent of the total enrolled militia personnel. Significantly, however, these trained bands would not constitute part of the general militia. In the event of war, they would be obliged to serve a three year enlistment with the Continental forces under the same terms as those of the regular soldiers. In order to ensure a high standard of readiness, trained band officers would hold an equal rank with corresponding regular Continental officers. They would also compete for promotion on the same basis.

Hamilton made token proposals for the reorganization of the general militia along the lines suggested by Washington, but contrary to the spirit of Washington's "Sentiments", he clearly did not intend that the militia would constitute the Nation's primary line of defense. Rather than the rationalized, revitalized militia envisioned by Washington, Hamilton's militia would remain a third rate local defense force to be called upon in the last resort. The primary burden of defense would be rested on the regular establishment and the highly trained Continental reserves.[15]

While attractive from the stand point of strict military efficiency, Hamilton's plan did not offer the social/political advantages of the Washington plan. Furthermore, it was inevitably regarded by the traditional Whig republicans as constituting a classic standing army. The provision for recruiting the trained bands primarily from cities was probably intended to maximize access to available manpower in the smallest area in order to facilitate frequent training.

It could not have been better deliberately calculated, however, to excite the apprehensions of the republican ideologs. Already deeply suspicious of the corruption they saw inherent in city life, the republicans regarded this organization as a bald attempt to recruit a standing mercenary army from the anonymous and apolitical urban poor. It was precisely such men, owing allegiance to none but their paymasters, whom despots had historically recruited to suppress the liberties of the people. These republicans had little doubt that the real purpose of such an army would be to suppress the militia, and enslave the people.

Washington immediately saw the economic disadvantages and political dangers posed by the Hamilton plan. He responded to a private letter soliciting his views on the plan (then before Congress) with the following observations:

> . . . I must beg leave to remark that the general outlines for the establishment of the National Militia do not seem to me to be so well calculated to answer the object in view as could be wished. . . . . I am fully persuaded that the . . . Train Bands formed of the Inhabitants of Cities and Incorporated Towns will not afford that prompt and efficacious resistance to an Enemy which might be expected from regularly established Light Infantry Companies, or a general selection of the ablest Men from every Regiment or Brigade of Militia . . . such an Establishment would, in my opinion, be more agreeable to the genius of our Countrymen.[16]

In June of 1783, the nationalists held temporary sway in the Continental Congress.[17] Given the temper of the times and the surge in Washington's prestige in Congress as a result of his handling of the Newburgh affair, Hamilton might have succeeded in passing his version of the peace establishment plan despite its controversial provisions. Four days after the plan was submitted, however, a mutiny by Continental soldiers of the Pennsylvania Line prematurely interrupted debate on the plan, and fundamentally altered the tone of discussion when it eventually resumed.

On 21 June, 80 enlisted soldiers of the Pennsylvania Line, with the tacit encouragement and assistance of their Captain and Lieutenant, marched from Lancaster to Philadelphia demanding the pay and emoluments due them prior to their discharge. In Philadelphia, they were joined by approximately 200 previously discharged soldiers. Together, this group seized the local arsenal, and demanded that the Pennsylvania State Council authorize them to elect officers from their ranks. They also let it be known that they intended to see "justice" done before they would disperse.[18]

Although the troops' demands and demonstrations were ostensibly directed at the state authorities, Congress interpreted their actions as being meant ultimately for themselves. A week earlier, Congress received an insulting letter from these same troops demanding their arrears. With mutineers standing on the lawn of the State House--in one wing of which Congress also met--an alarmed Congress sent a committee to the State Council to ask that the local militia be called out to suppress the mutiny. The Council informed this committee, however, that the militia--presumably in no hurry to tangle with well armed and trained troops--refused to interfere until, or unless, the mutineers actually committed some outrage against the civil authority.[19]

Congress remained in session until three o'clock while outside, some of the mutineers loitered about shouting insults, and sometimes pointed their muskets at the windows of the State Council chamber. Ominously, the rebels began receiving encouragement and incitements to action from a civilian mob which had gathered to enjoy the excitement, and many of the soldiers were growing obviously drunk from spirits purchased at a Tavern across the street. As the delegates nervously left the State House at the end of the day, they were jeered and threatened by several soldiers, but none were physically accosted.[20]

On 24 June, without reconvening, Congress abandoned Philadelphia and moved the Capital to Princeton New Jersey. Word reached the mutineers on the 25th that Washington had dispatched three loyal regiments to Philadelphia to suppress the insurrection. With this encouragement, Philadelphia belatedly called out her own militia. With little alternative, the frustrated soldiers returned to Lancaster and were immediately disbanded. The officers involved in the mutiny, facing the certainty of execution if convicted on charges of treason, fled the country leaving behind a bitterly defiant letter justifying their actions by blaming Congress' parsimony and neglect.[21]

Objective observers of the events of June 1783 agreed that local Pennsylvania politics had played at least an equal part with the soldier's frustrations over Congressional mismanagement in inspiring the mutiny.[22] To many republican ideologs, however, the incident provided, at last, tangible evidence of their darkest ideological expectations. Inevitably, the standing army had, just as in the first English Civil War, turned upon the civil authority and attempted to usurp the powers of government. That the mutiny involved only slightly better than a single company, or that other Continental troops had moved with dispatch to suppress it, was of little importance to the now revitalized republicans. The dilatorious behavior of the Philadelphia militia, and the contributions of the civilian mob, if remarked upon at all, could be dismissed as demonstrating the corruptive influence of urban decadence.

When debate on the peace establishment plans resumed in July, it met bitter opposition from a strong new republican coalition led by delegates Elbridge Gerry, David Howell and, Arthur Lee. Through various maneuvers they managed to stall a vote on the plan until August, when Washington himself was called to give testimony before Congress assembled, and where he delivered his (qualified) endorsement of the Hamilton Plan. In the wake of this testimony Congress resolved to resume debate on the issue in October. By September, however, the republican coalition had managed to link together several highly sensitive issues then pending in Congress, and effectively altered the basis of debate to terms unfavorable to the nationalist faction.[23]

The issue of finances had bedeviled the Continental Congress since the beginning of the conflict, and in 1783 the problem of the public debt was reaching a new level of crisis. The central problem stemmed from Congress' dependence upon the states for all revenue. Congress had no authority to tax in its own right and could do little but complain when the states failed to provide funds requested to defray the costs of the War. Lack of funds to pay the troops was the primary reason for the enlisted mutinies during the War, and was the major source of discontent among the officers at Newburgh.

During the dark winter of 1778, the morale and discipline of the Continental Officer Corps had reached a desperate low. In an effort to prevent the imminent resignation and departure of a large percentage of his officers, Washington convinced Congress, over the strenuous objections of the New England republicans, to vote pensions of half pay for life to any officer willing to serve to the end of hostilities. When the crisis passed, these pensions came under immediate attack by the radical republican element in Congress. During the renewed military crises of 1780, however, Congress felt compelled, reluctantly, to confirm the half pay resolution in order to pacify the increasingly beligerant officer corps.[24]

With the end of the War imminent in 1782, nationalists in Congress began to propose measures by which the pensions could be funded. They were immediately opposed by Elbridge Gerry's old New England republican coalition, now joined by several key Southern delegates. The debate rapidly became acrimonious with both sides accusing the other of the basest motives, and arrogating to themselves claims of a superior patriotism. It was the recognition that the promised pensions might never be provided which stirred some hot headed officers to action at Newburgh. In Congress, nationalists and Army advocates joined forces to attempt to place the Army on the long list of Continental public creditors.[25]

After lengthy, and often vicious debate, the republicans were forced to the galling conclusion that the half pay resolutions had been legally and properly voted. Cognizant of this weakness in their argument, and anxious to forestall the Army's designation as a public creditor (which would require a full payment plan supervised by the state courts), the republicans suddenly endorsed an old proposal by the Army advocates to commute the lifetime pensions to a one time stipend of five year's full pay. Cooler heads in the Army recognized that, given the public mood, and the chaotic state of fin es, this was probably the best renumeration they could hope to a   eve. The bitterness of the debate, however, was not forgotten by either group

The republican concern with the inclusion of the Army as a public creditor was not based solely on their distaste for being forced to pay the Continental officers for doing what they regarded as the officer's mere civic duty. The republicans were also apprehensive that adding the Army as a creditor would greatly improve the chances for passage of the National Impost Bill that was then pending. The Impost, a revenue tax on specified trade and imported goods, was proposed as a mechanism by which to supply the Continental Congress with a source of revenue independent of the states.

Nationalists, and many moderates, regarded the Impost as an essential measure if the Nation's debt was to be retired and economic order restored. The radical republicans, however, were always wary of granting the Central Government any save symbolic powers. They became highly suspicious of a proposal that would link an established military clique to a perpetual source of independent funds. Better, they reasoned, to pay these dangerously unreliable officers off and see the last of them.

For the officers part, many of the pro-pension arguments they used were not well calculated to enlist the sympathy of the average American citizen. With good reason, the officers pointed to the many sacrifices they had made in the service of their country; the farms abandoned and gone to seed, the interrupted educations, the trades grown stale or never learned. They also recounted their sufferings and privations endured on campaign, or in criminally inadequate winter camps. For these services they could justly demand fair compensation. Less sympathetically, however, the officers also complained, sometimes the more loudly, about their perceived loss of privilege and social position.[27]

Five or more years separation from their communities and normal lives had effected an often insidious change in the outlook of many of these men. In their daily regimental routines they were living the life of 18th century military gentlemen, a social position to which none but a very few of them could have aspired in the otherwise normal course of their lives. As these officers' pride in their military professionalism developed, so it tended to isolate them emotionally and politically from their civilian peers. Constantly afforded the deference due their military rank in camp, many of them came to expect it as their personal due.[28]

The officers' sense of isolation was exacerbated by the enhanced cosmopolitanism developed through long and close association with fellow soldiers from all the different states. As a result of their experiences and sacrifices, many officers began to view their personal patriotism as superior to that of the common citizen, or the increasingly despised politician. Perhaps most significantly, compared to the responsibility, excitement, sense of fraternity, and commitment to a great and momentous cause just experienced, civilian life looked dull, tedious, and banal. These attitudes made many officers apprehensive about returning to a civilian world wherein most would lose those distinctions which set them apart. General Arthur St. Clair was forthright in his assessment: "Officers cannot return to their former employments, their habits are too much changed."[29]

These arguments would not have generated much sympathy among the American yeomanry. In revolutionary America deference might be voluntarily bestowed upon notable or prominent persons, but it could never be demanded. A high regard for the virtues of hard honest labor was the enduring legacy of the Puritan heritage. What most civilians saw was a group of idle middle class officers taking on pretentious airs and demanding that the public treasury support them in a pseudo-aristocratic lifestyle antithetical to the basic precepts of the Revolution.

In September 1783, the Impost measure, which under the Articles of Confederation required the unanimous approval of the states before becoming law, was in serious trouble in several state legislatures. The republican coalition, sensing nationalist vulnerability, now demanded that debate on the Pension Commutation Act be reopened. They correctly accused the nationalists of attempting to pass the Impost in order to strengthen and perpetuate the power of the Central Government. They linked the peace establishment plans to this same design, and publicly charged the nationalists w   pting to establish a traditional standing army to be supported by an independent source of funds.[30]

The republicans suddenly charged that under the Articles of Confederation, Congress had no authority to maintain troops in peacetime. Certain republicans ensured that the least flattering documents from the Newburgh crisis were reprinted in the leading newspapers. All of the old arguments against half pay and commutation were dusted off and published as fresh revelations daily in sensational news accounts. Scathing articles painted the original half pay resolutions as a form of extortion by the Continental officer corps. The less scrupulous republicans charged that since continental officers had 10 times the opportunity of civilians for profiteering from the war, therefore there were 10 times as many profiteers among them. By way of dismissing the officers claims to compensation, one leading republican commentator falsely charged that: ". . . some officers left home in low indigent circumstances . . . all who return, return in affluence."[31]

Defenders of the officer corps struck back with articles explaining that the commutation payments were not demanded as a post-victory sinecure to support the officers in the style of gentlemen, but rather were restitution for services already rendered for which they had yet to receive compensation.[32] This argument was greatly weakened, though, when the republicans pointed out that all officers, including those who had joined the colors after Yorktown, and had therefore seen no significant active service, were eligible for the payments.

Commutation supporters inadvertently reinforced public cynicism when they defensively noted that Connecticut, who's delegation was among the most vocal opponents of any officer compensation plan, had been deliberately rotating state militia officers to the Continental service since 1782 in order to secure the greatest possible number of pensioners. Connecticut unapologetically replied that other states were doing it, and Connecticut was merely trying to secure her share of the public largess.[33] Instead of undermining republican credibility as the nationalists intended, however, this revelation only increased public hostility to the continental officers, tarring all, true veterans and opportunists alike, with the same brush.

Predictably, a public backlash against the officers' claims of special suffering rapidly materialized. Editorials posed the question; had not the private soldiers suffered as much or more than the officers? Why then, was there no demand to provide them with pensions? Had not the people also suffered at the hands of British depredations? Had they not endured the worst afflictions of the wartime economy? If the officers had suffered the interruption of their civilian pursuits, the editorialists claimed, then at least a benevolent country had provided them employment to see them through. This was more than was done for the civilian merchants and tradesmen. Many voiced the objection that, the Revolution had been fought to dispose idle "placemen" and hated aristocrats, not see them replaced by American substitutes.

The militia too, increasingly sensitive to slights from the Continental Army, began to demand recognition for their contributions to the victory. Had they not come forward repeatedly to run the same risks against the British as the Continental troops? Indeed, some asserted, theirs was the superior sacrifice since they had served without special compensation while maintaining their normal civilian responsibilities. Were they not even more entitled to pensions than the Continental Officers?

As historian Charles Royster phrased it: "The officers prated about their losses, but everyone saw men who had been nobodies before the war and now expected to live off the earnings of hard-pressed citizens and then claim superior patriotism in the bargain."[34] One private citizen spoke for many in an opinion to the editor of the New York Gazette: "I am willing that the soldier should stand on as good a footing as the citizen, but not better. . . ."[35]

The controversies raged on from the fall of 1783 to the spring of 1784 when, at last, public interest waned.[36] By then, it was clear that, however unpalatable, the half pay pensions had been appropriated through proper legal procedures. In this light, the Commutation act was seen to actually represent a financial bargain. The Continental officers troubles, however, were not over. In the midst of the commutation dispute, the officers found themselves embroiled in a new controversy.

In an effort to prolong that unique sense of identity and fraternity which had come to mean so much to them, Henry Knox organized an exclusive fraternity for officers of the combined Continental and French forces during the Army's last days together in the Newburgh camp. This organization, christened the "Society of the Cincinnati," was intended to ensure that the special bonds uniting these officers in wartime would remain after the peace. Knox envisioned that, like the legendary Roman general Cincinatus, the Continental officers would humbly return to their plows after saving the republic.

From time to time, however, the officers would meet so that the memories of their accomplishments, and those of that glorious Army collectively, would not be forgotten. In this way they could also perpetuate that sense of military selflessness and devotion to duty which might again be required someday to defend the nation. All officers who had held their rank on active service for three years, or who had been in uniform at the end of hostilities were eligible for membership. Members were to wear an eagle badge suspended by a ribbon as a mark of distinction. The Society planned to establish a fund to ensure no former officer would ever be reduced to the ignomy of poverty. In order that the goals and purposes of the Society should be perpetual, membership was to be hereditary, passing to the eldest son of each succeeding generation.[37]

Public criticism of the Society was immediate and violent. As noted, for many critics of the half pay controversy the officers worst crime was not their attempt to secure access to public money--a common enough, and often perversely admired ambition in the 18th century--but rather their claim to elevated social distinction based on their "superior" revolutionary service.[38] Aedanus Burke, writing under the barbed pseudonym "Cassius," published pamphlets nation-wide attacking the organization as a conspiracy to supplant republicanism with a new military aristocracy.

Burke alleged that the society had not been the work of Knox at all, but was created by Von Steuben--a Prussian aristocrat--to create a class of hereditary patricians who would ultimately oppress the people in the same manner as the old aristocracy of Europe.

Alarmed by the criticism, Washington, who was unanimously elected first President of the Society, solicited Thomas Jefferson's opinion on what measures might be taken to make the society more palatable and acceptable to the people.[39] In reply, Jefferson ventured his opinion that:

> The officers well meant affection might unintentionally create an organization hostile to the natural equality of man, and conducive to foreign influence, privilege, military distinction, habits of subordination, and the subversion of liberty.[40]

He went on to advise Washington to make a number of changes in the organization's by laws including: rejecting all donations from foreigners (a number of members were French officers), placing the Society's funds in the safe keeping of the state legislatures who would release them to be used for only the reasons expressly granted in the charter, terminating the plan to make membership hereditary, and to do away with the eagle and ribbon worn as a badge of distinction.[41]

Privately, Jefferson believed that Steuben and Knox were: "the leading agents among officers trained to monarchy by military habits . . . [who had proposed that Washington] assume himself the crown [at Newburgh]." Jefferson wrote that: "The epigraph of Burke's pamphlet was, "Blow ye the trumpet in Zion!"[42] Only Jefferson's deep affection and regard for Washington, and his knowledge of Washington's enthusiasm, and pride in the Society kept Jefferson from revealing his frank opinion of Knox's brainchild.

At the membership's first general meeting in Philadelphia in June 1784, Washington proposed that all of Jefferson's suggestions adopted. He expressed his reluctant resolve to abandon the Society and urge its disbandment if these measures could not be accommodated.[43] In the end, the National Committee of the Society agreed to adopt these proposals in principle, but forwarded them to the various autonomous state chapters as recommendations, rather than directives. By this stratagem Washington was able to retain his position as National President, despite the fact that none of the state chapters formally enacted any of Jefferson's ideas. In the event, the only change to be widely, though informally, practiced was an agreement not to wear the eagle badge in public except on special occasions and at funerals.[44]

In March of 1784, the Impost measure was decisively defeated when several New England states refused to ratify it. In open debate on June 2nd, bolstered by the Impost defeat, the implacable Elbridge Gerry delivered the most eloquent attack on a regular establishment yet marshaled by the republicans. In brief, he argued that if the Central Government were granted the authority to maintain troops in peacetime, this power would, "inevitably result in its [Congress'] resort to coercive means against the states."[45] Whereas if no regular peace establishment were formed, the increased responsibility on the militia would cause it to reform itself:

> We have so many brave and veteran officers to form and discipline the latter [militia], but if a regular Army is admitted, will not the militia be neglected, and gradually dwindle into contempt? and where then are we to look for the defense of our rights and liberties?[46]

Gerry went on to piously reassert the classic republican arguments against regular troops: "Standing armies in time of peace are inconsistent with the principles of republican governments, dangerous to the liberties of a free people, and generally converted into destructive engines for establishing despotism."[47] Many uneasy Congressmen must have recalled Massachusetts delegate James Lowell's lament when, in 1778, Congress granted Washington expanded authority to offer bounties to Continental recruits: "This was, in its beginning, a patriotic war!"[48]

Later that same day, Hamilton's objections not withstanding, Congress directed Henry Knox--since Washington's retirement, the senior officer on active service--to disband all of the remaining Continental regiments and discharge all save 80 soldiers and the appropriate corresponding number of officers. The mission of this tiny force would be to guard the military stores at West Point and Fort Pitt. The delegates then recommended that those states situated along the western frontiers collectively recruit a total of 700 men from their state militias to be enrolled in the federal service for one year, and situated in strategic posts along the borders to be determined later. In the event, the full compliment of state militia troops for this duty was never provided.[49]

In the course of eleven months, Gerry and the republican coalition had smashed the nationalist's momentum in Congress. In the process they had recaptured the revolution for traditional republican ideology. Historian Mercy Otis Warren, a close confidant of Elbridge Gerry's, immediately began work on her History of the Rise, Progress, and Termination of the American Revolution, which was not published until 1805, but was written primarily in the 1780s.[50]

Warren admitted that popular participation in the War had slackened after 1776, but, in the finest old Whig tradition, she attributed this phenomenon to the corrosive influence of decadent and easy living. The major American problem of the war as she saw it, was the ambition and greed of many of the American military leaders. In her interpretation it was the innate virtue of the yeomanry citizen-soldiers, whether continental or militiaman, who's fidelity to the purest republican ideals wrested victory from the machinations of their superiors, and who then, their civic duty completed, quietly returned to private life. This romanticized version of events was the one that most Americans wanted to believe, and so therefore, accepted.

The nationalists, though in retreat, were not defeated. The nationalist philosophy spawned its own historian. David Ramsay's History of the American Revolution (1789) provided a very different interpretation of events than Mrs. Warren's.[51] Ramsay concluded that at the beginning of the War, Americans had suffered from too much republicanism, and that a foolish reliance upon the virtue and self sacrifice of the individual had very nearly resulted in catastrophe. He argued that Liberty is relative, and that the Nation could not rely on the traditional militia model, but rather must accept the necessity for a professional military establishment if they hoped to retain their freedom from external aggression.

These divergent interpretations of the war's military experiences demonstrate the extent of the nationalist-republican schism that developed within the framework of traditional Whig ideology as a result of the Revolutionary conflict. Military policy and military philosophy were fundamental issues defining the nationalist and republican points of view. By 1784, the pedagogic nature of the debates had rendered these two positions nearly irreconcilable. The division of the people and their representatives into adherents of one or another of these contending camps helped set the stage for the most important public debate in the History of the United States; the struggle to ratify the Constitution. Indeed, Historian Walter Millis has argued that: "The Constitution was as much a military as a political and economic charter."[52]

Chapter One outlined the financial chaos, frontier troubles, and the Shays' Rebellion crisis which, in 1787, resulted in a convention to consider amendments to the Articles of Confederation.

71

Once a quorum had been assembled, however, James Madison, of the
Virginia delegation, proposed a startlingly more ambitious agenda. He
presented the Convention with a new plan of government which would not
amend, but

supplant the existing Articles. His "Virginia Plan " eventually became
the basic framework for modern United States Constitution.

It can be taken as a measure of the fear and anxiety felt by
the convention delegates about the condition of the Confederation, that
the momentous, and unauthorized, decision to abandon all discussion of
the Articles of Confederation and instead debate the Virginia, and
related plans, met with so little objection. Shays' Rebellion in
particular had shaken the normally imperturbable Elbridge Gerry. Upon
his arrival at the Convention he frankly told the assembly: "[He had]
been too Republican heretofore; [he was] still, however, Republican,
but had been taught by experience the danger of the 'leveling'
spirit."[53]

The Virginia plan made no specific provision for a standing
army. It was assumed by all, however, that the Federal government
would have to be endowed with some mechanism by which to enforce its
authority. Experience has demonstrated to the nationalists, and many
republicans, the truth of Thomas Hobbes' observation that: "Covenants
without swords, are but words."[54] Furthermore, with George Washington
sitting as Convention President, and one third of the delegates
veterans of the Continental Army, it was inevitable that the military
clauses of the Constitution would receive particular attention.

With memory of the ferociously violent debates of 1783/84 still
fresh in their minds, however, neither side was anxious to commence
debate on a subject that had every probability of creating an
immediate, irreconcilable impasse. Instead, delegates initially

72

concerned themselves with matters where common agreement seemed more certain, reserving the most contentious issues for later debate. When, at the very end of the Convention, the issue of the military establishment was at last taken up directly, the delegates had developed a clear concept of the checks and balances inherent in the emerging Constitution. They had also invested considerable time and mental energy in hammering out difficult compromises on other major issues, and were anxious to achieve compromise on this point lest so much effort go for naught. Nonetheless, the military provisions proved to be among the most highly emotional, and contentious issue debated.[55]

The use of the military to perform what are, today, commonly considered law enforcement duties was common in the 18th and 19th centuries. Under the concept of posse commitatus then prevailing, this was an accepted, indeed expected role for the military. The use of the militia for the maintenance of public order was (and remains) its most basic, and frequently executed mission. Early on, however, Madison concluded that the enforcement of Federal authority over a defiant state government by military force would not work. He reasoned that the invaded state would seize upon the invasion as a justification to sever all bonds with the Federal government, and a defacto state of war would then exist between the two. Furthermore, punishing an entire state for the actions of only a few recalcitrant officials did not seem either just or efficient.

The solution, Madison found, lay in his provision for an independent judiciary. Under the plan, the laws of the individual states would be bound ultimately by the common Constitution, as interpreted by the Federal Supreme Court. Officials who acted unconstitutionally, therefore, could be arrested and tried as individuals rather than attempting to punish their state collectively. Having thus neatly resolved the dilemma, Madison lost much of his

73

previous interest in the issue of a standing army.[56] The Continental
Army veterans, however, concerned as always with external, as well as
internal threats, remained adamant that the Constitution contain
measures to provide adequately for the common defense. They insisted
on including provisions that granted Congress the power:

> To Raise and support Armies. . . .
>
> To provide and maintain a Navy.
>
> To make Rules for the Government and Regulation of the
> land and naval Forces.
>
> To provide for calling forth the militia to execute the Laws
> of the Union, suppress Insurrections and repel Invasions.
>
> To provide for organizing, arming, and disciplining, the
> Militia, and for governing such Part of them as may be employed in
> the Service of the United States. . . .[57]

These provisions, penned in typically vague and noncommittal
style by Virginia Lawyer Edmund Randolph, did not specifically
establish a standing army, nor, however, did they rule out a peacetime
force.[58] They hinted at some federal involvement in militia
organizations, but failed to precisely define the relationship. The
temper of the times, and the wariness of both the nationalist and
republican factions made such generic legal phrases inevitable. To
have been more specific would have have required the inclusion of some
detail unacceptable to one or the other of the contending factions.

One republican delegate proposed that any regular army be
limited to two or three thousand men. To this, George Washington, in
one of his few recorded comments from the dais, is said to have
remarked in a stage whisper that such an amendment ought to include a
passage limiting any invader to the same number.[59] In a more practical
vein, George Mason, who, "hoped there would be no standing army in time
of Peace, unless it be but a few Garrisons," proposed that

appropriations for the Army's continuance ought to be limited to a
certain period to ensure its continued subordination to the civil
power.[60] This idea met with near universal approval and the clause
authorizing Congress to raise armies was amended to stipulate that
appropriations for the maintenance of the Army would be limited to two
years.

As it became apparent from the debate that the Constitution
probably would include no provision specifically barring a standing
army, Elbridge Gerry's republican instincts returned to their original
vigor. In a famous piece of wit he declared to his fellow delegates
that he was opposed to standing armies because: "A standing Army, is
like a standing member: an excellent assurance of domestic tranquility,
but a dangerous temptation to foreign adventure."[61] Joined by Mason and
a few other traditional republicans, Gerry was particularly concerned
with the clauses that could be interpreted as giving the Federal
government authority to organize and equip the state militias.

In answer to these concerns the nationalists reluctantly
compromised by amending a measure. ". . . reserving to the states
respectively, the Appointment of the Officers, and the Authority of
training the Militia according to the discipline prescribed by
Congress."[62] Gerry, however, was still not satisfied. Any Federal
authority over the militia, he insisted, would result in the "certain
destruction" of that venerable institution. Nationalists and
republicans made more compromises; the President would be the
"Commander-in-Chief of the Armed Forces," but the right to declare War
or invoke federal authority over the state militias would be reserved
to Congress. The clause in the Articles of Confederation limiting the
militia's term of active service to only three months in any one year
was carried into the Constitution, and Congress would reserve the right

to approve the appointment of all officers and officials proposed by the Federal Executive.

Ultimately, however, none of these safeguards was sufficient to overcome Gerry's opposition, and along with George Mason, he declined to sign the final document. The other delegates, though, were well pleased with their work, and a little in awe that so much had been accomplished so quickly.[63] Certain dissatisfactions remained of course. The nationalists were not entirely comfortable with the weak military provisions, and were especially disappointed at the failure to provide for meaningful militia reform. The republicans remained wary of the Army and it's potential to empower the executive with military force. Still, it was a better start, and offered a keener hope of succeeding, than any delegate had occasion to have expected at the beginning. It was assumed by the majority that necessary amendments could be made later.

Most delegates recognized that there would be a long, bruising fight ahead to win state ratification of the proposed Constitution. They must have ardently hoped that the checks provided against military power would be sufficient to prevent a repeat of the acrimonious debate surrounding the commutation dispute. Unfortunately for the nationalists, these hopes proved vain. Many provisions of the Constitution generated heated opposition, but the case for and against the military clauses were among the most emotional. It was these military provisions that were most starkly antithetical to traditional republican ideology, and they generated the greatest opposition by the republican "Anti-Federalists."

The Federalists' (as the nationalists, now a distinct political entity, were then becoming known) defense of the Constitution, and the anti-federalist attacks on it, were waged primarily in two venues. One was on the floor of the state legislatures, the other was a public campaign conducted primarily in the newspapers. Most surviving newspapers of the period were pro-federalist, and made no bones about this position in their editorials. The republicans complained bitterly that a biased press was advancing the position of a single faction.[64] A review of the literature, though, reveals that anti-federalist pamphlets, essays, and letters were widely reprinted and the consensus of scholarly opinion is that the Anti-Federalists' views received a largely fair hearing.

In addition to the ubiquitous Elbridge Gerry, leading republican opponents of the Constitution included George Mason, Richard Henry Lee, Patrick Henry, and George Clinton. Conspicuously absent from the debate due to his appointment as Ambassador to France was Thomas Jefferson, though his basic opposition to the Constitution is apparent from his collected correspondence.[66] Prominent members of the federalist camp were: George Washington, James Madison, James Wilson, John Jay, Noah Webster, and the persuasively eloquent Alexander Hamilton.

In the most famous defense of the Constitution, the Federalist Papers, "Publius" (Hamilton, Madison and Jay) devoted seven entries specifically to the military clauses. In the "Federalist No. 8," Hamilton, taking a leaf from the book of his republican critics, availed himself of the Whig historical traditional. Why had Ancient Greece, he wondered, not been forced to resort to a standing army? Because, he concluded, the economic circumstances of their tiny city states allowed all to participate equally in civic life. The fact that this was no longer possible in an "extended republic." he attributed to the changing circumstances of modern agriculture, industry and merchantilism. It was no longer possible, he argued, for one man to be all things at all times.[67] He believed that a regular army of the comparatively small size required for the protection of the United States could never become a serious threat to the people because:

> The smallness of the army renders the natural strength of the community an overmatch for it; and the citizens, not habituated to look up to the military power for protection, or to submit to its oppressions, neither love nor fear the soldiery: They [the people] view them with a spirit of jealous acquiescence in a necessary evil, and stand ready to resist a power which they suppose may be exerted to the prejudice of their rights.[68]

In response, the republican opposition trotted out all their traditional shibboleths, charging the Federalists with plotting to depose republicanism and install a strong executive that would effectively make of itself a monarchy. Denying that a Western crisis even existed, Patrick Henry decried the Federalist efforts to establish a standing army to guard the frontier. Henry claimed that the frontier security rationale for a standing army was a thinly veiled plot to undermine the militia and gradually supplant it with a purely federal military:

> A few regiments will do at first; it must be spread abroad that they are absolutely necessary to defend the frontiers. Now a regiment and then a legion must be added quietly; by and by a frigate or two must be built, still taking care to intimate that they are essential to the support of our revenue laws and to prevent smuggling. . . . [at the present time] Where is the danger? If sir, their was any, I would recur to the American spirit to defend us; that spirit which has enabled us to surmount the greatest difficulties . . . [but under the proposed Constitution] A standing army is to be kept on foot by which the vicious, the sychophantick, and the time-serving will be exalted, and the brave, the patriotic, and the virtuous will be depressed.[69]

Federalist James Wilson responded to such hyperbolic criticism in a more moderate vein:

> This constitution, it has been further urged, is of a pernicious tendency, because it tolerates a standing army in the time of peace. This has always been a popular topic of declamation: and yet I do not know a nation in the world, which has not found it necessary and useful to maintain the appearance of strength in a season of the most profound tranquility. . . . and no

man who regards the dignity and safety of his country, can deny the necessity of a military force, under the control, and with the restrictions the new constitution provides.[70]

Elbridge Gerry, however, was having none of it:

Though it has been said by Mr. Wilson and many others, that a Standing Army is necessary for the dignity and safety of America, yet freedom revolts at the idea, when the Divan, or the Despot, may draw out his dragoons to suppress the murmurs of a few, who may yet cherish those sublime principles which call forth the exertions and lead to the best improvements of the human mind.[71]

Noah Webster tried to bring the issue into perspective with a review of the Constitution's plan for a division of powers designed to limit the independence of the military:

. . . The principles and habits, as well as the power of Americans are directly opposed to standing armies; and there is as little necessity to guard against them by positive constitutional means, as to prohibit the establishment of the Mahometan religion. But the constitution provides for our safety; and while it gives Congress power to raise armies, it declares that no appropriation of money to their support shall be for a term longer than two years.[72]

The anonymous republican pamphleteer "Brutus" leveled an emotional and scathingly sarcastic reply to Webster's reasoning. In a transparent effort to rekindle the popular passions against the perceived haughtiness, elitism, and pretensions of the continental officers, he informed his readers that:

From the positive and dogmatic manner in which this author [Webster] delivers his opinions, and answers objections made to his sentiments--one would conclude that he was some pedantic pedagogue who had been accustomed to deliver his dogmas to pupils, who always placed implicit faith in what he delivered.[73]

The liberties of a people are in danger from a large standing army, not only because the rulers may employ them for the purposes of supporting themselves in any usurpation of power, . . . but there is great hazard, that an army will subvert the forms of the government, under whose authority they are raised and establish one according to the pleasure of its [the Army's] leaders.[74]

The incident at Newburgh had obviously made a deep impression on Brutus and he had not forgotten the officer's implied threat to refuse to be disbanded. He saw that incident as directly linked to other republican--nationalist controversies. Distorting and exaggerating facts in order to make them seem even more alarming, he reminded his readers of the "dangerous" events of 1783, and identified what he perceived to be suspicious and sinister connections between the events at Newburgh and the nationalist proposals at the Constitutional Convention:

> . . . Had the Commander in Chief, and a few more officers of rank countenanced the measure, the desperate resolution . . .[might have] been taken to refuse to disband. What the consequences of such a determination would have been, heaven only knows. The army were in full vigor of health and spirits, in the habit of discipline, and possessed of all our military stores and apparatus. They would have acquired great accessions of strength from the country. Those who were disgusted at our republican forms of government (for such there then were, of high rank among us) would have lent them all their aid. We should in all probability have seen a constitution and laws dictated to us, at the head of an army, at the point of a bayonet, and the liberties for which we had so severely struggled, snatched from us in a moment. It remains a secret, yet to be revealed, whether this measure was not suggested, or at least countenanced, by some, who have had great influence in producing the present [Constitution].[75]

Brutus launched by far the most blunt attacks by the anti-Federalist writers, but his opinions were doubtlessly shared by many more circumspect critics. His indictment of anti-republican "high officials" was a none to subtle assault on the character and suspected ambitions of Alexander Hamilton and other nationalists from the old Congress who had played prominent roles in shaping the proposed Constitution. These sentiments are indicative of the depth of the personal antipathy and mistrust held by some republicans for the nationalist leadership. Beyond the Constitution's specifically military clauses, the strength of the proposed national government in general caused anxiety among these republicans. Their objections indicate a lack of confidence that the scheme provided sufficient safeguards against what they regarded as a dangerous centralization of power in all its forms; military, financial, legislative, and judicial.

Many republicans condemned the innovation of a strong independent Executive (notwithstanding the universal recognition that Washington would be the first President) as a reckless invitation to tyranny. They defamed the proposed Senate, and claimed it masked an attempt to recreate a British-style House of Lords. Some charged that the concept of a bicameral legislature itself was an insidious attempt to introduce a hereditary aristocracy to the American Continent.[76] In the Whig historical tradition, the republicans most often expressed the issues of constitutional balance in terms of the balance between King and Parliament, as in the British model. In that sense, they feared the interests of an "Upper House" of Congress would more frequently coincide with those of the Executive than with those of the people.

Ultimately the question came down to one of power. How could sufficient power be gathered to suppress the forces of anarchy, or aggression, yet be rendered incapable of infringing on the liberties of the people? Traditional Whig ideology held that for a true republic to function, it must necessarily be limited to relatively small districts, or at the most, a state. Only in this way could legislatures be truly responsive to the will of the people, and loyal to their best interest. Even limited to areas of this size, there were significant problems as the events of Shays' Rebellion and other Western insurrections had shown. At the heart of the issue was the question of whether the authority of the individual state, or the Federal Government was to be supreme.

Under the Articles of Confederation, government had been arranged to favor the authority of the states. Article II of the Confederation stated that: "Each state retains its sovereignty, freedom and independence, and every Power, Jurisdiction, and Right, which is not by this confederation expressly delegated to the United States in Congress assembled."[77]   This was a formula for an extremely lose association of independent states, and it was this extreme separatism that confounded nationalist efforts to field larger Continental forces, or to impose order on America's chaotic finances during the Revolution. After the war, matters became even worse due to the states distrust, or disinterest in all save parochial affairs.   It was this ingrained parochialism that the nationalists and their moderate allies were so desperately trying to overcome.

Towards that end, James Madison hit upon the concept of the "extended republic" which he contrasted to traditional republican notions of democracy thus:

> . . . It [republican hostility to federalism] seems to owe its rise and prevalence chiefly to the confounding of a republic with a democracy--and by applying to the former reasons drawn from the nature of the latter. The true distinction between these forms . . . is, that in a democracy, the people meet and exercise the government in person; in a republic, they assemble and administer it by their representatives and agents. A democracy, consequently, must be confined to a small spot. A republic may be extended to a large region.[78]

The concept of the extended republic developed by Madison and others is an elegant and complex piece of political philosophy who's full appreciation lies outside the scope of this paper. In brief, Madison was extending the concept of elected representation far beyond that which had previously been considered possible. Delegates to the Continental Congress had been appointed by their legislatures, not directly elected by the people. A state's delegation was expected to represent the people only indirectly by acting on the instructions of the elected state legislature.

Under Madison's new concept of national representation, Representatives and Senators were to be elected directly to their offices by local constituencies, providing an uninterrupted link directly from the national level of government to the provincial districts. Madison's concept divided government into discrete state and national spheres, which significantly degraded the sovereignty of the state government within the Federal Union. The debates on various schemes of electing, or selecting these representatives proved the most lengthy, and hotly contested issue during the convention.

A major, if frequently unarticulated objection of many of the Anti-Federalists was this requirement, implicit in the Constitution, to surrender a large proportion of the individual state's autonomy. Many leading republicans did not accept, or did not approve of, Madison's extended republic. They were skeptical that an organization as removed from the common perspective and perceptions of the people as a national government could retain those simple virtues upon which they believed true liberty depended.

From that view point, the actual military effectiveness of the local militia was not as important for the republicans as their symbolic role as the state's independent troops. For the republican ideologs, a totally separate militia was necessary to be the, "ultimate guarantor of the peoples liberty," and balance state independence against potential federal ambitions.[79] The hyperbolic use of the term "tyranny" in much of the Anti-Federalist literature then, must also be seen as an ideological metaphor for less cataclysmic concerns about the erosion of the states' rights.

Republican ideology notwithstanding, the failure of the the Articles of Confederation to produce an effective union deeply disquieted a majority of the people. The civil disorders between 1784 -1787 were proof for most eastern voters that, Madison's judicial analysis aside, the government must, in extremis, have some means of physically enforcing its authority. The people were as quick to see the dilemma of how to protect themselves from the potential ambitions of their protectors as were their leaders. They, however, were less concerned about maintaining philosophical purity than many of the Anti-Federalists. These citizens concern was to effect practical solutions to the problems without sacrificing their basic prerogatives.

Despite the heroic rhetoric, it was clear to many private citizens that the existing militia system was dangerously weak. For those in and near the Western areas, this was no matter of mere symbology. It was Western farms that were burnt by Indians the militia could not suppress, Western trade goods that were seized by insurrectionists. They wanted effective protection immediately, and had grown less concerned about the steps necessary to achieve it. Therefore the Constitution's scheme to provide national assistance in organizing the militia, while simultaneously allowing the states to retain significant authority over training and the appointment of officers, was attractive providing the primarily local allegiance of these forces could be assured. In the "Federalist No. 24," Hamilton addressed this point by arguing:

> The power of regulating the militia, and of commanding its services in times of insurrection and invasion, are natural incidents to the duties of superintending the common defense. . . . Where, in the name of common sense, are our fears to end, if we may not trust our sons, our brothers, our neighbors, our fellow citizens?[80]

Republican objections remained tied to the notion of the militia as the champion of the people's rights against a remote and unrepresentative government. Republicans expected that the states would have no control over the recruitment or employment of the regular regiments. Republican ideology assumed that a system which included a regular establishment would automatically seek to suppress the local

84

militia. It presupposed a strong central government essentially alien
to the interests of the provincial citizens.

Gradually, however, people came to understand that the proposed
Federal Government would be composed of representatives elected
directly by, and therefore responsible to, local constituencies. They
also learned that the power of the central government would itself be
divided between the Legislature, the Executive, and the Judiciary, and
not autocratically exercised. They discovered that the traditional
militia system was to be retained alongside a regular establishment,
and that final authority over the leadership and training readiness of
the militia would be reserved to the states. As these concepts became
widely understood, popular opposition to the Constitution rapidly
declined.

In some measure this was due to the ideological inconsistencies
and obvious absurdities in the republican arguments. On one hand,
republicans professed an absolute reliance upon, and faith in the
essential virtue of the provincial militiaman. On the other, they
expressed concern that the exposure of these same men to any degree of
Federal influence would result in their rapid transformation as the
willing agents of tyranny. To be sure, inconsistencies were to be
found within the various defenses of the Constitution as well, but few
that could not be reconciled by a careful review of the document.

Ultimately, what sunk the Anti-Federalists was their failure to
provide reasonable alternatives to the federalist proposals. The
Federalists were offering concrete solutions to problems posing a
tangible threat to all of the country. The republicans could only fall
back on the same threadbare arguments against centralized powers that
had been offered before the Revolution began. Even the most ardent
republican sympathizer had to admit that on many occasions the old
militia system had failed to respond adequately to the demands of

85

crisis. The Antis were offering no viable reforms, no systemized alternative concept of national defense. They were merely reiterating the same republican rhetoric that had proven inadequate during the war with Britain. The Federalists were offering something, while the Antis could only play devil's advocate. There was, however, one final anti-federalist objection that could not be so easily dismissed.

The most egregious, and least satisfactorily explained omission in the Constitution was its lack of a bill of rights. Most of the state constitutions contained such a bill and it was widely considered to be an essential declaration of the individuals inviolable rights. George Mason, author of the Virginia Constitution's bill of rights, was particularly critical on this point, as was Thomas Jefferson.[81] Some Federalists responded, rather lamely, that since the new government derived its powers directly from the people, such a proviso was unnecessary—a hold over from the social contract between ruler and subject. The republicans were adamant, however, that an explicit enumeration of the limits of governmental power was an indispensable guarantee of minority rights. Even James Madison was uncomfortable with this oversight and pledged that he would campaign to so amend the Constitution immediately after its adoption.

As legislators came to accept that a bill of rights would be added, many republican sympathizers confidently assumed that it would contain provisions expressly prohibiting or limiting standing armies in peacetime, endorsing the traditional role of the militia, and clearing up other questionable elements of the federal scheme.[82] This belief greatly mitigated the strength of much republican objection. Armed with this understanding, states began to ratify the Constitution during the winter of 1787-88, a majority of the state legislators having come to agree with Benjamin Franklin's assessment:

. . . I confess that there are several parts of this constitution
which I do not approve, but I am not sure that I shall never
approve them. For having lived long, I have experienced many
instances of being obliged by better information, or fuller
consideration, to change opinions even on important subjects, which
I once thought right, but found to be otherwise. . . . Thus I
consent, Sir, to this constitution because I expect no better, and
because I am not sure that it is not the best.[83]

Thus the political struggles of the 1780's defined two distinct
theories of American defense of a pattern still identifiable today.
The Nationalist/Federalist theory corresponded to the general outlines
established by Washington at the end of the Revolution. It called for
a professional standing army substantial enough to meet the exigencies
of most credible external or domestic threats. The Army would be
composed of long service volunteers, highly disciplined, and maintained
in a constant state of operational readiness. These regulars would
police the frontier, enforce federal authority in the territories,
deter attacks by hostile Indians or neighboring colonies, and provide a
military model for the militia.[84] During peacetime, the Army would
maintain sufficient supernumerary strength to provide cadres in the
event that the number of regiments had to be rapidly expanded to meet
an emergency. The Army would be supported by a regular Navy who would
also have the mission of protecting the nation's commerce.

Under the Federalist concept, the state militia would retain,
as its primary role, the maintenance of internal security, and domestic
tranquility. Selected elements of it, however, would be subject to
muster into the Federal service for limited periods of time during
emergencies. For this purpose they would be federally regulated,
armed, and organized. Discipline and training were to conform to
standards established and proscribed by Congress.

In the event of invasion by a major power, the selected
militia, supported by the regular Army and Navy, would conduct the

initial resistance, while regular Army cadres raised and trained forces sufficient to defeat and repel the enemy. An alternative to the selected militia concept favored by some Federalists, was a federally recruited Army Reserve Corps. Under this proposal the traditional militia's role would be relegated exclusively to local defense and public order.

The federalist theory also called for the establishment of a nationally sponsored military academy to impart to the officer corps a high degree of technical expertise in military engineering, maintain professional standards of proficiency in all duties, and to suffuse high standards of professionalism throughout the entire military establishment. These forces were to be collectively supported by the maintenance of military stores and equipment in national magazines, arsenals, or depots located so as to insure their immediate availability during a crisis. Though not expressly stated, the regular Army would also, in the final extreme, provide the Federal Government with a credible ability to enforce its authority against defiant state or local governments.

The republican theory, though never emerging as fully formed and articulated as did the Federalist concept, essentially placed the entire burden of national defense on the militia alone. Relying upon America's isolation from Europe, and the comparative weakness of her neighbors to protect her from any serious foreign threat, this theory regarded the existence of regular troops as a greater internal threat, than any identifiable external challenge. The immediate availability of professional forces would also be an unacceptable temptation to "foreign adventure" by a strong central legislature, or executive, enabling government to prosecute foreign wars without the consent of the people.

The presence of a standing army was seen as pernicious to the
effective development of the militia because it eroded civic virtue,
encouraging the decadent habit of paying others to fight for them. A
regular force was undemocratic because it was not a balanced reflection
of the society it served. It would not share the common interests of
the community and would act to further its own interests. The
professionalism which set it apart, would transform the standing army
into a powerful competing faction within the government. Furthermore,
even discounting the social and political threats, a standing army
would be an unnecessary drain on national finances, money which could
be better used to retire the debt, or to make civil improvements.[85]

Republicans believed that the mass of the people, armed,
organized militarily, and regularly exercised would be sufficient to
cope with routine local, or regional threats. In addition to the arms
and accouterments provided by the individuals themselves, it might be
necessary to provide some limited support, such as artillery, from a
few regional military depots, but in the main, communities would be
expected to shoulder the burden of supplying their own equipment. If a
few full-time frontier garrisons were necessary, they could be provided
by volunteers from the existing militia, rotated on an equitable basis
among the various community units. A small professional Navy to
enforce the tariff laws, and patrol the coastal commerce lanes might be
tolerated because it was commonly understood that navies posed no
threat to civil authority.[86]

In the unlikely event of a major conflict, the width of the
oceans, and the poor routes of communication within the continent would
provide sufficient time for larger scale preparations. As had been
done in the Revolutionary War, the Congress could then create the
necessary organizations, appoint the national leadership, and intensify

89

the training programs to achieve the level of proficiency required. In the absence of such a threat, such preparations were needlessly expensive and unnecessarily dangerous.

In the underlying patterns of these divergent defense concepts, the respective social ideologies of nationalism and republicanism can be identified. While they shared the same basic goals; an America in which the people were free to enjoy the blessings of life, liberty, and the pursuit of happiness, they differed fundamentally as to how this was to be best accomplished.

At its root, republicanism concerned itself primarily with the rights of the individual against the state. It relied upon what it believed, or hoped, was a uniquely American public virtue. A virtue that was as yet fragile, and required protection from the forces of repression and tyranny. Republicans contended that the people must not be allowed to fall into the habits of decadence and corruption that had reduced the populations of Europe to docile subservience. Republicanism regarded political power with extreme suspicion, and shared it jealously with governmental authority. Republicans regarded social justice and equality as the "natural state" of mankind.[87] They believed, however, that this natural state had been historically repressed by the greed and venality of a powerful few. The ideal society then, was one in which the power of the government was minimized.

Federalism took a more pessimistic view of man's basic nature, and a more optimistic one about government's potential for beneficence. Hamilton reminded his readers that along with their noble characteristics, men were also: ". . . ambitious, vindictive, and rapacious."[88] Federalists sought to make a virtue of self-interest by setting the natural factions off against each other, effecting a balance between them. The federalist goal in the Constitution was to maximize individual liberty, while creating enough checks upon man's deleterious tendencies to prevent collapse into extremes of either anarchy, or despotism. Federalists put little store in the perfectibility of man's character, and so sought mechanistic solutions to prevent the encroachment of selfish ambition. They hoped to accomplish a government strong and efficient enough to defend the nation from external and external threats, yet fettered by enough internal restraints to keep its internal powers in check.

Republicanism and federalism represented two differing approaches to the attainment of American ideals. The separate military philosophies evolved by these groups reflect this divergence. In this dichotomy can be identified certain enduring ideological tenants which influence debate on America's military establishment to the present day. These ideas, and their republican, or federalist roots may be distinguished by the application of three criteria and corollaries:

1. <u>Attitudes Towards Government Military Power</u>:

Republican attitude toward military power was characterized by an extreme mistrust and suspicion of governmental military authority, and preference for a more democratized, less centrally controlled military organization even at the expense of military efficiency, or professionalism.

Federalists exhibited an abiding faith that, to be effective, government must be possessed of an effective, centralized, military capability. They possessed a strong commitment to the organizational efficiency and professionalism of the military, and a skepticism that these traits could be adequately developed in decentralized militia or reserves.

2. <u>Concept of the Relationship of the Military to Society as a Whole</u>:

The republican concept was characterized by the belief that to be legitimate, the military must be representative of the broader society from which it springs. That an appreciation of the true value of liberty can only be achieved through sacrifice for its attainment. They viewed the primary purpose of military service as a means of fostering civic and republican virtue. They remained highly suspicious of the ultimate loyalty and motivation of highly disciplined regular forces. Republicans regarded enthusiasm and commitment to basic republican ideals as preferable to institutional discipline.

Federalists were primarily concerned that the military be capable of fulfilling its responsibility to provide an effective defense. They were not concerned with the demographic make-up of the standing, or reserve forces. Federalists remained committed to traditional concepts of rigid military discipline and stoicism. They did not view the military itself as a necessary reflection of the society, but rather as an organizational instrument of a representative government. Federalists fostered the concept of the military standing "above politics". They regarded a centralized military establishment as nurturing an expanded sense of national unity among the separate states.

3. Attitude Towards Military Preparedness:

Republicans regarded a high state of peacetime readiness as a dangerous invitation to internal repression, or external aggression. They resented expenditures of public money in the absence of a tangible, immediate threat. They regarded requests for military appropriations to "deter" potential threats, as unnecessary, and suspected they were primarily motivated by a professional military desire to further its own interests. They believed that an armed, and ideologically motivated citizenry was the best guarantor of national survival, and rendered standing forces unnecessary.

Federalists believed that a high degree of military preparedness is critical to effective resistance against foreign aggre   n. They adhered to the theory that a constant state of preparedness is the most effective deterrent to conflict, and comprised a superior long term financial, and moral economy. They were convinced that military skills and proficiency are highly perishable, and require constant exercise to be retained. They believed that an efficient, "respectable," military enhances the prestige and effectiveness of the nation.

It is important to recognize that in 1788 the adherents of these ideological cor   s   d not yet coalesced into coherent political parties. When, over the course of the next decade, such parties emerged, republicanism became identified with the Jeffersonians, or "Republican-Democrats" in opposition to the "Federalist" majority. When this happened many formerly prominent supporters of the these respective movements changed sides. James Madison eventually allied himself with Jefferson, and became a bitter rival to his old comrade Alexander Hamilton. Patrick Henry, Richard Henry Lee, and Robert Yates all became Federalists.[89]

In the process, many of the basic tenants of these movements transitioned from philosophy to partisan political dogmas, and positions hardened, often irrationally, as a result. Over time, however, as the first political parties rose to prominence and then declined, these tenants once again escaped the exclusive claim of any single party and have endured as constituent (albeit often contradictory) elements in a vaguely defined American "Creed." They are part of a traditional American ideology, but as political scholar Samuel P. Huntington has pointed out:

> . . . In the American mind these ideas do not take the form of a carefully articulated, systematic ideology in the sense in which this term is used to refer to European belief systems. . . . They

constitute a complex and amorphous amalgam of goals and values, rather than a scheme for establishing priorities among values and for elaborating ways to realize values.[90]

Chapter six will explore the way in which these "amorphous goals and values" are still active in shaping Americans attitudes about the military establishment, and how they have created parallels between the modern debate about force structure and defense policy with those just examined. First, however, Chapter five will describe the consequences of republican--federalist rivalry over the development of a permanent American military establishment, and its influence on the American military tradition.

CHAPTER 5

THE DEBATES 1790 TO 1796

The ratification of the U.S. Constitution in 1788 by 11 of the 13 states (North Carolina and Rhode Island did not ratify until early in Washington's first administration, and only then under duress) was a tremendous victory for the Federalists (emerging as a result of the struggle for ratification as a coherent, and discrete political party). The provision for a standing army was now firmly established in the basic law of the United States. If, however, supporters of a strong regular system expected rapid establishment of forces along the lines of Washington's 1783 proposals, they were sadly disappointed.

On April 6 1789, The First United States Congress, assembled in New York, finally achieved a quorum and was able to officially convene the electoral college which confirmed the election of George Washington as President. Washington was inaugurated in a small ceremony on 30 April. The first congressional session was dominated by the requirement to organize, virtually from scratch, the Federal Government provided for under the new Constitution. Other pressing matters were measures to temporarily fund the fledgling government until permanent revenue legislation could be enacted, and debates on the Bill of Rights amendment proposals that had been envisioned during the ratification process.

It was not until 12 September that the Senate confirmed Washington's appointment of Henry Knox as his Secretary of War, and not until the 29th, the very last day of the first session, that the Congress finally got around to adopting into Federal service the 80 regulars and 700 volunteer militia that had been garrisoning the frontier posts under the old Confederation. This same measure appropriated funds for the maintenance of a standing army (drawn largely from rotating volunteer militia) of 840, of whom only about 672 were then actually in service.[1] This was a significant reduction from the 2,600 thought necessary by the President.

That the state of the nations military preparedness was a priority on Washington's agenda is evidenced by an address he made to Congress on 7 August of that year:

> . . . I mean some uniform and effective system for the militia of the United States. It is unnecessary to offer arguments in recommendation of a measure on which the honor, safety and well being of our country so evidently and essentially depend; but it may not be amiss to observe that I am particularly anxious it should receive as early attention as circumstances will admit, because it is now in our power to avail ourselves of the military knowledge disseminated throughout the several states by means of the many well-instructed officers and soldiers of the late [Continental] Army, a resource which is daily diminishing by death and other causes. To suffer this peculiar advantage to pass away unimproved would be to neglect an opportunity which will never again occur, unless, unfortunately, we should again be involved in a long and arduous war.[2]

Unspoken, but apparent in Washington's statement was his conviction that the way to preclude future involvement in long and arduous wars, was to be adequately prepared to deter them. It is also apparent that Washington had given thought to ways to repair the schism that had developed between the nationalists and the republicans and he hoped that by merging the veterans of the old Continental service into the revamped militia, he could reconcile the one to the other, as well as perpetuate their knowledge of the military art.

Unsuccessful in the first session, Washington planned to press the militia issue early in the second congressional session. His diary for December 18, contained this entry: "Read over and digested my thoughts upon the subject of a national militia from the plans of the militias of Europe, those of the Secretary of War [Henry Knox] and Baron Von Steuben."[3] On December 19, he wrote: "Committed the above thoughts to writing in order to send them to the Secretary for the Department of War, to be worked into the form of a Bill, with which to furnish the Committee of Congress which has been appointed to draft one."[4]

Presumably these thoughts formed the basis for the proposal known as the Knox plan of 1790, which was submitted to Congress in January of that year.[5] This plan was a relatively minor variation on one submitted to the old Congress by Knox in 1786. It reduced the total required number of training days, but retained Washington's concept to divide the militia into various age categories, and the establishment of separate light companies. Washington made it clear that in order to achieve a basic agreement to the concept of a nationally based militia, he would be willing to reduce the required training days still further, and negotiate other details as well.

While national defense may have been the first priority for Washington, it is evident that this was not the case for most other legislators. Even James Madison, a fellow nationalist, showed little sense of urgency when he wrote to Thomas Jefferson at the end of January 1790: " The business of Congress is as yet merely in embryo. The principal subjects before them are the plans of revenue and the militia."[6] In consonance with this lack of urgency, the Knox plan was referred to the Committee of the Whole on January 21, where it languished without debate until April 26. On that date it was referred to the new Committee on National Defense chaired by Elias Boudinot. On July 1, Boudinot finally introduced a militia bill that was based on an entirely different principal.[7]

It was much more than mere indifference, however, that doomed the Knox plan. Knox was not noted for his literary skill, and some complained that the proposed plan was too long and difficult to understand. Worse, Knox had tactlessly endorsed his plan to Congress under a cover letter which explained that it was intended to defend the country from *internal* as well as external threats, and that it provided the central government with a "strong corrective arm." This caveat further irritated tender republican egos still smarting from their unsuccessful opposition to the new Constitution. As historian John McAuley Palmer phrased it: "At a time when they [the Congress] were appending a Bill of Rights to the Constitution of the United States, they were not inclined to equip the Federal Government with a 'strong corrective arm'."[8]

Knox, Washington, and the other military reformers also failed to adequately forestall the tremendous influence of local jealousies, and partisan politics. State militias were full of locally elected, or appointed officers who were not about to surrender their positions, and the attendant social cachet, without a struggle. Cynically or sincerely, these groups fervently enshrouded the issues in the traditional republican arguments to resist a national militia system. The February 10th edition of the Gazette of the United States included this letter from a Connecticut citizen:

> By the returns of the Militia of the State of Connecticut, there appears to be six brigades, thirteen regiments of infantry, six of cavalry . . . amounting in the whole to thirty thousand effective men, well officered and appointed, and completely armed: most of the regiments were reviewed last month, and are generally in a neat uniform. A degree of emulation pervades officers and privates to excel in the military art, that does honor to them as freemen, and as citizens of a republic, who are determined to support the constitution and government of the country, without the aid of a standing army, or an expensive national militia.[9]

Connecticut, it should be remembered, was not one of the larger states, yet it could field (on paper) the equivalent of three 18th century divisions. The pressing financial difficulties of the nation, combined with the strong residual anti-military sentiment in their districts, made it easy for the representatives in Congress to accept such defenses of the existing militia system uncritically. Despite the influence of Washington's personal interest and prestige, the majority of legislators were highly reluctant to impose sweeping military reforms. General Benjamin Lincoln neatly summed up his estimation of the people's mood in a February Letter to Knox:

> Though it would make ours the Strongest militia in the world, the people will not adopt it here if I know Massachusetts . . . The Expense . . . the burden on Masters, calling the youth indiscriminately . . . subjection to a draft for a service of three years, etc. will be magnified here and dim the bill.[10]

After being reported on July 1, 1790, Boudinot's revised bill was returned to committee where it languished for another five months. On December 13, it was reported again, but after only brief debate, was returned to committee on January 4, 1791. It stayed there until 1 November, when the House created a new committee, dominated by Federalists, which returned it for debate on 21 November. The Committee of the Whole, however, managed to delay debate for three additional months. When, at length, discussion finally commenced on the measure, it fell immediate victim to the Federalist versus Republican--Democrat animosities which were again inflaming passions within the Legislatures.[11]

Most of the debate focused on the bill's details, but a significant amount was devoted to the, by then familiar, republican ideological arguments. Once again the liberal histories of Greece and Rome were reviewed, along with the dire lessons of the English Civil Wars. Revisionist histories of the Revolution, conveniently overlooking the role of the Continental Regiments, were brought forth. Finally, for the first time, the remarkable achievements of the citizen National Guards in the then unfolding French Revolution were cited.

Remarkably, this period of equivocation over the uniform militia proposals was coincident with the darkest period of conflict between the Federal Government and the Frontier Indians. So dire appeared the threat from these Indian nations to Western settlers that, in April 1790, Senator Butler of South Carolina declared that if Federal military help were not sent to Georgia, the citizens of the Western counties would seek help elsewhere, presumably from Spain.[12] Though this assertion was denied by the remainder of the Georgia delegation, incidents with the Southern Creek Indians were on the increase.

In the North West, Brigadier General Josiah Harmar led a failed punitive expedition against the Shawnee Indians in the fall of 1790. In November of 1791, General Arthur St. Clair's punitive expedition against the Shawnee was smashed in a costly and humiliating defeat. These disasters, as well as pressure from other Western constituencies, frightened Congress into increasing the size of the regular army three separate times in twenty two months.[13] It did not, however, result in the Federalists' ability to marshal the political will in Congress to reform the militia system.

This peculiar circumstance can, to some degree, be accounted for by the hardening of Federalist and Republican--Democrat (herein after to be referred to as simply Democrats) positions within Congress that was alluded to earlier. It was in this period of American history that coherent political parties emerged. Whereas, formerly, like-minded men might band together in "factions," these tended to be issue specific, and votes were cast by individual legislators largely on the basis of what they perceived to be a given measure's unique merits. Certainly, ideological convictions played a dominant role in reaching these conclusions, but for most men these ideological strains had not yet coalesced into a comprehensive political vision. In the early 1790s, however, party lines began to be drawn upon more purely ideological grounds.

In 1790, republicans were becoming especially suspicious of the motives, and ambitions of leading Federalist Alexander Hamilton. During the Constitutional Convention, Hamilton had proposed an alternative plan of government to that of James Madison's. It was the opinic of many of the old republicans that this plan was a thinly veiled attempt to impose on America, a government that would have been, in effect, a centralized elective monarchy. True or not, Hamilton undoubtably feared governmental authority less than most of his peers, and was an unapologetic elitist. And Hamilton, along with several other kindred Federalists, had the President's ear.

The Democrats gradually became convinced that Hamilton was attempting to establish, through a liberal interpretation of the Constitution, what he failed to accomplish at the Constitutional Convention. In reaction Jefferson, the newly converted Madison, and other republican leaders, banded together into a Democratic opposition party. It is indicative of both the times, and the complexity of Jefferson's character, that he saw no inconsistency in these actions and his continued performance of duties as Washington's Secretary of State. It seemed to the Democrats of 1792, that it was possible democracy in America might not long survive.[14]

While forced by the practical necessity of the western situation into expanding both the size, and the role of the regular establishment, the nascent Democrats in Congress must have been even more reluctant to further increase the military authority, and power of

the Federal Government. Especially a government so influenced by
Alexander Hamilton. Finally, in open debate on 5 March 1792, the
remaining provisions that would have effected meaningful Federal
control over the state militias were removed, leaving the bill an empty
shell which essentially provided the states mere suggestions on militia
organization. On 6 March this revised version passed out of the House
by a vote of 31 to 27.[15] On 29 March, after minimal Senate debate, it
passed into law as the Unified Militia Act of 1792.

Historian John K. Mahon has pointed out the danger of
oversimplifying the significance of the party vote on the Militia Act.[16]
His analysis shows that based on known party affiliations, the vote was
badly split and no definitive pattern can be ascribed to it. Still,
more Federalists were in favor of it than opposed, and more Democrats
opposed than in favor. Further, it was decidedly republican arguments,
delivered by such practiced ideologs as Richard Henry Lee, that
succeeded in removing the most important clauses.[17] It is reasonable to
assume from the evidence that many Federalists voted for the final
version of the bill in hopes of its eventual improvement. Many
Democrats probably also saw in it an effective way to demonstrate their
concern over the western situation, without actually committing
themselves to any dangerous military experiments.

Democratic reaction to passage of the Militia Bill was
predictably positive, and many touted the legislation as a significant
advance, as this letter to the National Gazette dated 8 May 1792
attests:

> A militia system, the true and equal guardian of freedom and a
> free country, which at several preceding Sessions experienced
> insurmountable obstacles, has at the present, been at last
> accomplished.[18]

Federalist opinion, as reflected in the <u>Gazette of the United</u> <u>States</u>, however, was more cynical:

> The Militia Law will probably seem a feeble system to many persons versed in military affairs. The great difference of the militia laws of the several states is such, that some will improve and others perhaps run retrograde in consequence of this law of the United States. But amendment will be made from time to time, and it is to be hoped that eventually this act will not be one of the least perfect parts of the national system.[19]

Overshadowed by the Unified Militia Act of 1792, but of at least equal importance, was another measure passed by the House a month later, but which actually became law a week earlier. Known as the "Calling Forth Act," it was adopted so that the clauses authorizing the central government to "call forth" the militia into Federal service could be implemented.[20] This act gave formal authorization to the President, in time of emergency, to summon to Federal duty as much militia as he deemed required by the situation. It also confirmed Presidential authority to command and discipline the militia while on Federal duty without having to clear such directives through state authorities.

Republican features of this act included two important provisos. First, while militiamen on active Federal service could be held to the same articles of war as regular troops, they could be tried only by courtsmartial composed of other militiamen. The second formally limited the length of time a militiamen could be compelled to perform Federal service to three months in any one year. This second provision eventually resulted in the collapse of the traditional militia system because, in time, it led to a preference by the Federal military authorities to rely upon non-militia volunteers when mobilizing manpower, to the exclusion of the general militia.

In contrast to the Uniform Militia Act, the Calling Forth Act specified penalties to be imposed for failing to comply with

Presidential authority. That these ostensibly complimentary acts,
should receive such different treatment at the hands of the same group
of legislators speaks eloquently of the dilemma confronting the
Democrats in 1792. They were torn between their mistrust of the
Hamilton Federalists on the one hand, and on the other, the necessity
to field some manner of effective military force in the West. They
were attempting, in essence, to have it both ways, and they would pay a
stiff price for these inconsistencies later during the War of 1812.
For the moment, however, the Western crisis remained the dominant
consideration.

In the absence of meaningful militia reform, Henry Knox
continued to push for enlargements of the regular establishment. In
the Spring of 1790, having received reports that agents of the Spanish
government were inciting trouble among the southern Indians, Knox
requested an expansion of the standing army by an additional 1,000 men
in order to garrison new posts along the southern frontier.[21] The
debates over this proposition revealed the extent of Democratic
suspicion and personal antipathy for the Federalists. Seconding a
speech on the dangers of standing armies by Richard Henry Lee,
Pennsylvania Senator William Maclay declared:

> Give Knox his army, and he will soon have a war on hand;
> indeed, I am clearly of the opinion that he is aiming at this even
> now, and that, few as the troops that he now has under his
> direction, he will have a war in less than six months with the
> Southern Indians.[22]

Maclay was a noted curmudgeon and little liked by any of his
fellows. His statement met with derision by the Federalist members of
the chamber, but his accusation of conspiracy nonetheless reflected a
real, and increasingly widely held Democratic belief. The Democrats
were successful in limiting this increase of forces to 500 additional
troops, but following the ineffectual Harmar expedition in 1790, Knox

succeeded in wining approval to increase the regulars to a strength of 2,000.[19]

After St. Clair's rout on the Wabash, Washington had had enough of combined militia/regular organizations. He petitioned Congress for authority to raise a regular force of 5,120.[24] This force, soon designated as "The Legion of the United States," trained and disciplined to a professional standard, and supported by a force of carefully selected mounted Kentucky volunteers, became the instrument by which Major General Anthony Wayne crushed the Shawnee and allied Indian nations at the battle of Fallen Timbers in 1794. This action, combined with the collapse of the Whiskey Rebellion, effectively ended the military troubles along the western frontier until the War of 1812.

The combination of the shock of St. Clair's defeat, and Washington's personal prestige were sufficient to win congressional authorization for the Legion legislation after only perfunctory debate. Later, however, during the discussions on possible reductions of the military establishment following the decisive military victories of 1794, motives other than military necessity were impugned to the efforts to increase the regular establishment. True to form, Senator Maclay, this time joined by several other of the more radical Democrats, again espoused his anti-Federalist conspiracy theories.

According to Maclay's version of events, Knox knew that the National Militia Bill would encounter stiff opposition, and deliberately included within it unacceptable provisions to which he then "stuck fast" in order to dead-lock the debate. While Congress was preoccupied with these issues, so Maclay's theory ran, Knox proceeded, with "art and address of ministerial management," to sneak through appropriations to increase the standing army.[25] He privately believed that the administration had deliberately and clandestinely provoked

Indian trouble in the North West as an excuse to raise a large standing army with which it would then "awe the citizens into submission."[26]

Such inflammatory statements serve to underscore the depth and ferocity of the political conflict between the Federalists and Democrats. It is doubtful, however, that very many Jeffersonians believed these conspiracy theories to be literally true. As propaganda such stories were eagerly circulated, but when it came to a vote in 1796, there was surprisingly little Democratic support for abolishment of the regular forces.[27] In May of 1796, Congress passed an act disbanding the Legion, and reorganizing it into four regim   of Infantry, two companies of light dragoons, and a corps of artillery.[28]

After the passage of this measure, much Democratic bombast and extreme rhetoric to the contrary notwithstanding, no serious effort was ever again made to completely eliminate the standing regular army.[29] Twelve years of unrelenting Indian warfare in the North West had demonstrated to all but the most extreme Democrats the necessity to keep a responsive force permanently in the field. Instead, the debate shifted after 1796, to arguments about the appropriate size of the regular army, and its role vis-a-vis the organized and volunteer militia.

Further evidence of the hard headed practicality at work alongside the ideological dogma of Democratic thought can be found in the military amendments to the Bill of Rights. During the Constitutional ratification debates in 1787-88, it was widely assumed that when a Bill of Rights was appended to the Constitution, it would include provisions limiting the size and authority of a peacetime standing army. When, however, the second amendment was eventually passed, it concerned itself exclusively with the rights of the militia to "keep and bear arms." Indeed, contrary to expectations during the original ratification debates, there is no record of any substantive debate having taken place that even considered formal constitutional restrictions on the military clauses.

Perhaps this was indicative of a fuller understanding of the appropriations power invested in the House of Representatives, or possibly it reflects apprehension over the western crisis. In either event it demonstrates the shift in Democratic ideology away from traditional, reflexive republicanism toward a broader acceptance of limited centralized powers. This change in Democratic attitude became boldly apparent when, in 1800, Jefferson defeated John Adams in the Presidential election, and brought to power the nation's first Democratic administration.

A detailed account of the deepening rivalry between the Federalists and Democrats for the remainder of the decade lies outside the scope of this paper. The military significance of this period, which encompassed the so called "Quasi War" with France, was the attempt by President John Adams and the Federalists to greatly increase the nation's military in preparation for, what they believed to be imminent hostilities. Jefferson, an avowed Francophile, accused Adams of blatant militarism, and of colluding with the hated Hamilton to impose a military dictatorship. So desperate and passionate did the contending parties in this imbroglio become, that at one point in 1798, Adams believed that open civil war between Federalists and Democrats was probable.[30]

Adams regarded this possibility so seriously that he managed to ram through Congress the infamous "Alien and Sedition Acts," measures which gave the Federal authorities sweeping powers to suspend civil rights, and impose military law if necessary to suppress insurrection. These hugely unpopular measures, the enormous expense of the military expansion program, and incessant quarreling and intrigue within the

107

ranks of the party combined to displace the Federalists in the election of 1800. Within a few years of this defeat, the Democrats had effectively destroyed the Federalists as a viable political party.

Thomas Jefferson, however, was no longer the same man who had penned the Declaration of Independence. While on appropriate occasions his rhetoric could still ring with all the ideological fervor of the "Spirit of '76," the intervening 24 years had taught him the practical realities involved in governing a fractious country surrounded by hostile neighbors. Among his first legislative measures was a bill not to reduce the regular establishment, but rather to increase it.[31]

In a memorandum intended to define "the essential principles of our Government, which ought to shape its Administration," Jefferson, heretofore among the staunchest supporters of the pure militia concept, now wrote that; "a well-disciplined militia, [is] our best reliance in peace and for the first moments of war, till regulars may relieve them."[32] This statement demonstrates that Jefferson had absorbed both the military lesson of the American Revolution, and, perhaps, the experiences of Revolutionary France, more thoroughly than he had been previously willing to admit. Jefferson's Democratic Secretary of War Henry Dearborn harbored even stronger Federalist military views. Writing in 1798 during the height of the War scare with France he confided:

> This country should abandon any idea of depending upon Militia for prosecuting a war. They may be useful on sudden emergencies, but without better discipline than I ever expect to see, . . . it is hardly possible with almost any numbers, to oppose with success, a well appointed regular Army of only fifteen or twenty thousand men. The moment when war with France is considered as inevitable, the United States must raise at least one hundred Regiments. . . . More is to be feared from the want of information and discipline in the officers of the Militia generally, than from want of discipline in the privates.[33]

Jefferson, and his successor James Madison exhibited contradictory attitudes toward the concept of regular forces. They frequently denied that the very type of man who would become a regular soldier could even exist within the framework of American liberal society, while simultaneously employing these theoretically non-existent soldiers on important tasks all over the Frontier.[34]   Without attempting to analyze this psychological phenomenon further, Jefferson and Madison certainly possessed that form of selective political dogmatism which allowed them to conclude that a power dangerous in the hands of an opponent, was rendered not only safe, but indispensably necessary when in their own possession.

The defections of prominent republicans such as Richard Henry Lee, Robert Yates, and even Patrick Henry to the Federalist Party during the early 1790s also acted to weaken the influence of traditional republican ideology on the evolution of Democratic thought. By 1800, both federalism, and traditional republicanism had collapsed as coherent political movements. Many of their basic ideologies, however, have survived to influence consciously, or unconsciously the politics, policies, and public attitudes of every generation of Americans from that time to our own. The next chapter will demonstrate the ways in which these ideologies can be seen to be influencing the current national debate on a revised American defense policy.

CHAPTER 6

THE DEBATES 1989 TO 1994

In the October 29, 1993 edition of the National Catholic Reporter there appeared a column by Jesuit Professor Robert F. Drinan under the following headline: "Military establishment threatens U.S. Democracy."[1] Friar Drinan opened his essay with the quote from Dwight Eisenhower in which the President warned against the dangers of the "Military Industrial Complex." Drinan went on to present quotes from the Declaration of Independence, in which George III is condemned for keeping standing armies in peacetime, the 1784 Congressional resolution declaring standing armies incompatible with republican ideals, and a quote (taken out of context) from George Washington's farewell address condemning "overgrown" military establishments as "inauspicious to liberty."

Drinan's purpose in the piece is to present his contention that in the 50 years spanning World War II and the Cold War, America has become dominated by militarism. He condemns the expenditure of billions on America's defense budget, and believes that the continued existence of a large military establishment encourages American politicians to seek military solutions to problems, however inappropriate. He concludes by calling his readership to challenge this situation:

> . . . The generals will offer and perhaps urge their services. If a president is pressured by national and international opinion to "do something," he will be tempted against his better judgment to pick the military option. . . . Opposing the military mentality is clearly countercultural. But it is one of the most serious demands on the Catholic community at this awesome moment of profound transition in American history.[2]

Drinan presents his views using his authority as a
representative of the Catholic Church. Significantly, however, he does
not use the moral authority of the Church to frame his arguments.
Rather, he confidently enumerates the anti-military ideologies of
traditional American republicanism. Drinan clearly expects that by
phrasing his thesis in terms of these commonly held American ideological
principles, he will sway a larger audience than by limiting his appeal
to Catholic doctrine alone.

Drinan's piece demonstrates the remarkable resilience and
longevity of American republican ideals. The origin of these
ideologies in the European Enlightenment movement predated the formation
of America as a separate nation. Their role in inspiring the American
Revolution, enshrined them as fundamental elements of the American
Creed. Yet the impracticality of fully realizing these principles, and,
at the same time, developing workable and effective governmental
institutions, has been the fundamental dilemma in American politics.
Political scientist and historian Samuel P. Huntington described this
inherent tension thus:

> In America, ideology in the form of the principles of the
> American Creed existed before the formation of a national community
> and political system. These principles defined the identity of of
> the community when there were no institutions for dealing with the
> other countries of the world. It was assumed that the foreign-
> policy institutions, like other political institutions would reflect
> the basic values of [these principles]. Yet precisely these
> institutions--foreign and intelligence services, military and police
> forces--have functional imperatives that conflict most sharply and
> dramatically with the liberal-democratic values of the American
> Creed . . . [whose essence is] opposition to power and concentrated
> authority. . . . This conflict manifests itself dramatically in the
> perennial issue concerning the role of standing armies and
> professional military forces in a liberal society.[3]

Huntington goes on to point out that prior to the twentieth
century, America was able to avoid the full implications of this
conflict because of its relative geographic isolation and its

preoccupation with domestic issues. To be sure, the issue of supremacy between the citizen-soldier, or military professionals animated considerable political discussion during the nineteenth century. But in the absence of an immediate foreign threat, the advocates of an enlarged regular military invariably fell victim to the inbred American distaste for professional military institutions, and the economists in Congress who balked at the expense.[4]

The Spanish American War in 1898, however, marked a water shed for American military policy. The campaigns in Cuba and the Philippines were the U.S. Army's first significant involvement outside the North American Continent. In 1898 the Army was expanded from a token frontier constabulary of 25,000 officers and men, to 65,000. This force was backed up by an additional 250,000 volunteers called from the states.[5] After the conclusion of the campaigns against Spain, the insurrection in the Philippines prevented Congress from disbanding this organization as was traditional following American wars.

To suppress the insurgency Congress decided to expand upon an experiment that had been conducted with good success during the 1898 campaigns. Rather than call for state organized volunteers, as was done for previous operations, Congress directed that 35,000 volunteers "from the country at large" should be raised. This new pattern of "National Volunteers" further reduced the involvement of the state governments in military policy.

In the wake of the numerous mobilization problems and supply scandals revealed by the War with Spain, President McKinley tasked his Secretary of War, Elihu Root, with formulating proposals for comprehensive Army reform. Root's investigations, and the associated Congressional hearings, produced a national debate on defense issues similar in magnitude to that conducted after the Revolution. Advocates of a strong standing army and those championing the militia once again squared off against each other.

The resentments felt by many army officers toward penurious congressional policies that kept the Regular Army in a state of near destitution for most of the 19th century, combined with their professional derision for the inefficiency and "amateurism" inherent in the militia and volunteer system, caused many of them to advocate the termination of the traditional reliance on citizen-soldiers. Many hoped to replace it with a system of national reserves on the European model.[6]

Conversely, many veterans of the Volunteers (notably Theodore Roosevelt) acquired a low opinion of the intelligence and abilities of the regular officers whom they encountered in Cuba and the Philippines. They were joined by the powerful National Guard lobby and states-rights advocates in successfully blocking proposals for a "National Reserve."[7] In place of the purely national programs, Congress adopted a proposal sponsored by Representative Charles W. Dick (a General in the Ohio National Guard). This legislation, known as the "Dick Act of 1903", superseded the old Uniform Militia Act of 1792. The Dick Act perpetuated the militia as the Army's primary organized reserve, but Secretary Root succeeded in wringing from it major concessions that the 1792 legislation had lacked.

Under the new law federal subsidies to support state troops were greatly increased. In order to secure this money, however, states had to agree to submit their militia organizations to periodic inspections by regular army officers, and to maintain these units at specified strengths. The law also specified that militiamen must attend a minimum of 24 drills per year, as well as participate in 5 days annual training. In 1908, an addendum was added which established an Office of

Militia Affairs within the War Department, and, significantly, lifted the restriction on the number of months in a year the President could call the militia into Federal service. This last provision was nullified, however, by a 1912 Attorney General ruling denying the President the authority to employ the militia outside the Continental United States.[8] This decision had the effect of derailing the momentum of the militia reform movement.

The exigencies of persistent guerrilla warfare in the Philippines, the necessity to maintain sizable garrisons in America's newly acquired overseas territories, and the continued reliance on the restrictive militia system, combined to dramatically expand the peacetime Regular Army. In 1903, Congress fixed the number of officers at 3,996 and authorized the President to set the enlisted strength anywhere between 60,000 to 100,000, at his discretion. This same legislation established an Army General Staff. Collectively, these measures advanced the nation's reliance upon the professional military to an historically unprecedented degree. It seemed to many involved in these issues as if the dreams of Washington and Hamilton had at last been realized.[9] Yet the traditional influences of republicanism, though in temporary eclipse, were far from extinguished.

The convulsion of the Great War in Europe in 1914 caused the U.S. to consider its state of military preparedness with renewed urgency. The Republican Party (the modern, conservative leaning, political organization of that name--sometimes referred to as "Big R Republicans"), with the poorly concealed support of the General Staff, adopted preparedness as a partisan political issue to use against President Woodrow Wilson and the Democrats.[10] Initially, Wilson retained a purely traditional liberal view on the subject:

It is said in some quarters that we are not prepared for war. What is meant by being prepared? Is it meant that we are not ready

upon brief notice to put a nation in the field, a nation of men
trained to arms? Of course we are not ready to do that; and we
shall never be in time of peace so long as we retain our present
political principles and institutions. . . . To defend ourselves
against attack? We have always found means to do that, and shall
find them whenever it is necessary, without calling our people away
from their necessary tasks to render compulsory military service in
time of peace.

. . . We must depend in every time of national peril not upon a
standing Army nor yet upon a reserve army, but upon a citizenry
trained and accustomed to arms, . . . a system by which every
citizen who will volunteer for the training may be made familiar
with the use of modern arms.[11]

In these passages Wilson demonstrated his belief that
traditional American mobilization methods could cope with the new
European mass armies. The European mass armies were predicated upon a
system of peacetime conscription and compulsory military service. These
expedients were the only possible way of developing the huge numbers of
trained reserves necessary to rapidly mobilize effective fighting forces
numbering into the millions. In view of the manpower possessed by the
Europeans, the issue of how to attain an adequate reserve became the
focal point for the Army preparedness debate through 1916.

Under increasing pressure from the Republicans, and with an eye
to the 1916 election, Wilson's administration worked through 1915 to
develop a program acceptable to the preparedness critics. The plan
eventually forwarded by the General Staff called for a force numbering
1,500,000 at full mobilization strength. This would consist of a
500,000 man regular Army, and an equal number of part-time individual
reserves to be designated as the "Continental Army" (in effect, a
Federal Army reserve), plus another 500,000 men designated to begin
training immediately upon mobilization who would provide individual
replacements to the mobilized forces as the fighting progressed. The
state militias were disregarded as being of no utility to the federal
authorities.[12]

The plan immediately generated a storm of protest by the National Guard/States-Rights block in Congress. These were soon joined by traditionally minded Democrats who, in the words of historian Walter Millis: "[saw that] behind the whole plan there stood the shadow of conscription and of the great, Federally commanded standing army which the nation had historically feared and rejected."[13]

James Hay, powerful Chairman of the House Military Affairs Committee, suggested an alternative to the Administration's plan. Rather than substitute a Federal Reserve for the Militia, he proposed that the Militia be modified to become a Federal Reserve. Under this scheme, the Federal Government took over the full responsibility for equipping, organizing, and paying the militia units. Governors and State Adjutants General would be required to maintain their forces at a standard of training and efficiency established by the War Department. Most significantly, regular Army authorities would now have the right to set the standards for the appointment of officers, and could refuse to recognize the commission or the authority of any state appointed officer they deemed unqualified or unsuitable.[14]

The President and most members of Congress found this a more politically palatable solution than the Continental Army plan. After discussing it with Wilson, Representative Hay released the outlines of the plan to the Press. The day following this release, in an odd show of anti-republican temper, Wilson's Secretary of War, Lindley Garrison, confiding his objections to the Hay proposal to the President, revealed that he privately harbored some very federalist attitudes about national defense:

> There can be no honest or worthy solution which does not result in national forces under the exclusive control and authority of the national government. . . . The very first line of cleavage . . . is between reliance upon a system of state troops, forever subject to constitutional limitations, . . . or reliance upon national forces, raised officered, and controlled by national authority. . . . The

116

difficulty does not arise out of the government being unable to take over these [state] troops in time of war, but arises out of its inability under the Constitution, to have the essential unity of responsibility, authority and control in the raising, officering, training and governing of its military forces.[15]

With some modifications, the Hay proposal eventually passed into law as the National Defense Act of 1916. The Act at last formally adopted the name "National Guard" which had been used informally for 50 years.[16] It created an American land force consisting of four components: the Regular Army--with an authorized strength of 175,000, the Federally regulated National Guard--composed of the state militias, an Army Reserve--to be officered primarily by officers trained in the ROTC detachments at the Land Grant Colleges, and a "Volunteer Army"--an ambiguous organization to be raised exclusively during wartime.

This legislation was perhaps the most important single piece of military legislation in American history. It represented the final abandonment of the militia's traditional role as a direct counterbalance to the standing army, and reflected (despite Secretary Garrison's views to the contrary) the triumph of the Federal over state military authority. After 133 years, Washington's vision of a national militia had finally become a partial reality. Hereafter, the National Guard would retain its distinctive role of providing local part-time troops to assist and support the state governors, but, despite many legal challenges extending into the 1980s, it would ultimately remain firmly subordinate to Federal authority.

Mobilization later in 1916 to meet the crisis along the Mexican border demonstrated that even with these sweeping reforms, sufficient manpower could not be raised to meet the actual demands of active service. When America declared war against the Central Powers in 1917, the 1916 legislation was superseded by an act to, "Increase Temporarily the Military Establishment."[17] This new measure expanded the size of the Regular Army and the National Guard, and provided for an additional "National Army" with a projected starting strength of 500,000 to be raised by a selective service draft. It was intended that this force would be expanded by an additional 500,000 as soon as sufficient training cadres and facilities could be established.[18]

Adopted with surprisingly little debate, this act fundamentally altered the basic assumptions upon which the United States had traditionally based its military establishment. From the adoption of this measure on the eve of World War I, through Vietnam, the United States, during times of national emergency, became reliant upon a standing army manned and reinforced by civilian conscripts provided through the selective service system.

This reliance upon a draft army largely superseded the National Guard's role as a Federal reserve, and allowed the professional military establishment to marginalize the Guard's importance to the Federal Government for the successful prosecution of armed conflict. The Guard retained its utility as state troops, however, and their powerful political lobby and propaganda value as a link to America's citizen-soldier tradition insured the Guard's survival as an institution. Nevertheless, until after the Vietnam war, the Guard was little regarded, and minimally supported by the regular Army.

The movement by the Nixon administration to end the draft and return to a dependence upon an "All Volunteer Army" in the early 1970s revived the long dormant debate between the supporters of pure military efficiency, and the adherents of republican ideologies. The existence of the draft (in nearly continuous operation since before WW II) had obscured much of the traditional Democrat-Federalist ideological tension. The social upheavals of the 1960s, however, created an environment of vigorous--sometimes violent--debate on virtually every facet of government. A major impetus to these debate came from the violently anti-military sentiments held by a large proportion of the draft age population, and the liberal wings of the dominant political parties.

Since the eclipse of the National Guard and the state Volunteer system in 1917, many liberals had come to regard the practice of staffing the Army with short-term conscripts as having the unintended, but welcome benefit of providing that hedge against professional military hubris once provided by the citizen soldier. They regarded the selective service system as the logical evolutionary development of the old militia concept.[19] By rotating large numbers of primarily civilian-minded young men through the military every two years, and by diluting the suspect regular officer corps with reserve officers trained in the civilian Universities, any autocratic ambitions harbored by the professional military could be effectively thwarted.

The radical anti-militarists of the 1960s, however, took a much more traditionally republican position in their opposition to conscription. These radicals often framed their arguments in terms that would have been entirely familiar to any of the participants in the First Continental Congress. Liberal spokesmen lifted wholesale the Enlightenment philosophies synthesized in Tom Paine's The Rights of Man, and applied them in support of the "Anti-Establishment" Peace movement.[20] This period witnessed a strong revival of eighteenth century liberal thought. In historian Michael Howard's analysis, the revival of these views, combined with the erosion of popular respect for the authority of the state, provided certain influential liberals with a simplistic political mantra for the perfection of society:

> The whole "war system" was contrived to preserve the power and the employment of princes, statesmen, soldiers, diplomats and armaments manufacturers, and to bind their tyranny ever more firmly upon the necks of the people. Break the power of the Establishment, introduce a political system in which popular interests were truly represented, demolish all artificial barriers to international

119

intercourse, and the whole nightmare would quickly disappear. . . . Peace was therefore fundamentally a question of the establishment of democratic institutions throughout the world.[21]

To liberals of this persuasion, conscription, and by extension involuntary participation in foreign wars, was fundamentally undemocratic. The passion inspired by this attitude was vividly captured by the Vietnam protest slogan "Hell No, We Wont Go!" To another group of thinkers, however, the conscript Army was viewed as a preferable instrument of liberal democracy to a professional volunteer force.

The prospect of conversion to a large professional Army deeply offended the democratic sensibilities of educator Harry A. Harmion. In 1971 he published a slim volume entitled, The Case Against A Volunteer Army, in which he brought to bear all the traditional republican objections to military professionalism.[22] Harmion protested that:

> . . . a voluntary army would further isolate the military from the rest of the American society. . . . There are some who feel that Fletcher Knebel's political fantasy, 'Seven Days in May' [a novel about a military coup d'etat in America] described a situation which could, under certain circumstances become a reality in this country . . . isolation from the body politic, super-patriotic militarism, and collusion between the military and the nation's defense industries are already present under the draft. Under a voluntary army they would be exacerbated.[23]

> If we had no draft, but rather a volunteer force partially hidden from view, and one clearly not representative of the whole society, would there then not be a similar national clamor for getting out of Vietnam? It is, of course, unlikely that there would, and in this sense the creation of a volunteer army may be said to undermine democratic processes in America.[24]

There were also, of course, contemporary authors of a federalist bent who argued in favor of conversion to an all volunteer force precisely because of the professional limitations they saw inherent in the conscript Army. T. R. Fehrenbach, in his study of the Korean Conflict This Kind of War, published in 1962, urged the adoption of a

professional army as the only way to cope with the unique military
demands of the Cold War:

> Less than a year after fighting ended in Korea, [North] Vietnam
> was lost to the West, largely because of the complete repugnance of
> Americans toward committing a quarter million ground troops in
> another apparently indecisive skirmish with Communism. . . . The
> policy of containment cannot be implemented without professional
> legions. . . . Reservists and citizen-soldiers stand ready, in every
> free nation, to stand to the colors and die in a holocaust, the big
> war. Reservists and citizen-soldiers remain utterly reluctant to
> stand and die in anything less. None want to serve on the far
> frontiers, or to maintain lonely, dangerous vigils on the periphery
> of Asia. There has been every indication that mass call-ups for cold
> war moves may result in mass disaffection.[25]

Another major issue surrounding the discontinuance of the draft
centered on the question of an all volunteer force's ability to recruit
sufficient soldiers to maintain an adequate force structure.[26]
Embedded within this issue were questions about disproportionate
representation of minorities, and an unprecedented reliance on women to
fill the ranks. Characteristically, conservatives tended to view this
change in demographics as having potentially negative repercussions for
efficiency and preparedness. Liberals, on the other hand, expressed
concern that poverty and other forms of social inequality would
effectively "draft" the under classes into the military because of a
lack of other options.

For both conservatives and liberals the issue of the loyalty of
an army composed of the poor and uneducated was a cause for concern.
Liberals feared that soldiers who enlisted for pay would be loyal only
to the highest bidder. In a letter to the New York Times, John W.
Finney expressed his fear that: ". . . The nation might be acquiring a
mercenary force drawn from the lower classes that future political
leaders can use for military adventures."[27]

Likewise, there were allegations from some black activists that
conservative preoccupation with the minority issue was predicated more

on racist anxiety than a genuine concern for equitability of service. As representative Shirley Chisolm testified before a House Armed Services subcommittee:

> All this talk about a volunteer Army being poor and black is not an indication of "concern" for the black and the poor, but rather of the deep fear of the possibility of a black Army. Very few people desire to verbalize the underlying fear and anxiety of a large number of black men trained in the military sense in a nation where racism is rampant. Individuals who are upset over black power rhetoric shudder at the idea of a whole Army of blacks trained as professional soldiers.[28]

Whatever the motivation, the debate about the demographic make-up of the Army corresponds neatly with the 2nd of the criteria developed in Chapter Three; Attitudes Toward the Relationship Between the Military and Society. The liberal position demonstrated an enduring republican ideal that the composition of the military should reflect that of the society from which it springs. It also provides evidence of the extent to which professional soldiers, even when enlisted from the citizenry into the national army, were regarded by many as little better than mercenaries. The conservative positions, conversely reflect the traditional federalist preoccupation with pure military efficiency and disregard for slavish adherence to abstract notions of demographic representation.

In spite of these objections, the All Volunteer Force became a reality in 1973. Its introduction restored the importance of the National Guard as a trained reserve. Without the ability to rely on the selective service system to create a continuously replenished pool of trained manpower, the Army adopted the "Total Force" policy in 1974. This program was designed to integrate Guard and Reserve forces with regular forces on a routine basis for training, and not merely, as was the historical case, during wartime.

In 1976 the "Round Out" program reorganized most of the Army's active duty divisions such that, upon mobilization, their third brigades would be provided by a designated National Guard unit. The majority of the Army's logistic support capability was transferred to the Guard and Reserves at the same time. Under these massive reorganizations it became virtually impossible to commit the Army to any significant operation without at least a partial reserve mobilization. These developments returned American defense policy to a posture analogous with that of the 1780s. Once again America became reliant upon a combined force mixing Regulars, Guardsmen, and Reservists to mount combat operations.

The aftermath of the Cold War found the United States confronting a disparate and nebulous set of dangers that was also analogous to the 1780s. The dissolution of the Warsaw Pact and the collapse of the Soviet Union removed the immediate global threat against which America had been arrayed since 1950. In the absence of an immediate, obvious, and unequivocal enemy, many Americans began agitating for rapid massive reductions in military forces.

The collapse of the Soviets did not, however, result in instant unalloyed peace. The break-up of the Soviet Empire set off a a host of small, but vicious nationalist, and ethnic conflicts among the newly independent eastern European countries. Released from the restrictions of the superpower struggle, dozens of long simmering regional disputes burst into open hostilities. Furthermore, the emergent Russian republic, as well as several of the larger successor states, retained massive conventional forces, and a nuclear arsenal that continues to hold the continental United States at risk.

These continuing dangers to American interests and population are underscored by America's involvement in the 1990-91 Persian Gulf War, The Somali Intervention, the Islamic terrorist attack on the World

Trade Center, and the increasing involvement in the Civil War in former Yugoslavia. These events have engendered a brisk, national debate on defense, and foreign policy issues. In these debates we can see at work the continuing influence of the ideological principles which animated the debates of the 1780-90s. By applying the established criteria the historical parallels and philosophical influences between these two periods can be easily identified. The most closely parallel among these criteria is number three, Attitudes Towards Military Preparedness. The conflict between conservative and liberal ideology on this issue reveals obvious similarities to the peace establishment debates.

The issue of restructuring the military, and what constitutes an acceptable level of military preparedness was a major subject during the 1992 Presidential election. Both candidates professed to be committed to ensuring that the United States retain a strong defense capability. In several key areas, however, they differed markedly as to how this should be best accomplished. These differences were especially apparent on the issue of the role of the Guard and Reserve Forces in a reduced force structure.

President Bush favored a plan developed by his Defense Secretary, Dick Cheney, which would reduce the overall strength of the Military, but retain the basic structure, and relative proportions of Regular, Guard, and Reserve forces that existed at the time of the Persian Gulf War. To accomplish this, it would be necessary to make cuts in existing National Guard strength of about 150,000 personnel. This proposal met strenuous objection from National Guard Lobby, and exacerbated existing tensions between the National Guard and the Bush Administration resulting from the controversial handling of Guard units during Gulf War. In an attempt to temper these objections, President Bush contributed an article in the October 1992 issue of the National

Guard magazine in which he explained his position and stated his
commitment to the Guard as an institution:

> As President, I could not have acted decisively in the Persian
> Gulf without full confidence in American armed troops--both active
> and reserve. Each day of the Gulf conflict, I heard countless
> instances of their gallantry. . . . Yet the 21st century will
> present different challenges. Future risks to our security will be
> marked by ambiguity and rapid change--not the relative certainty of
> the past. One asset of experience is an appreciation of history . .
> . [it explains] why we must realign the size and shape of the Guard
> and Reserve to meet our new national security requirements in a
> world different than the 1980s.[30]

Democratic candidate Bill Clinton adopted a different vision for
the restructured defense establishment. He foresaw an expanded role for
the Guard in the Nation's defense. In the same issue of the National
Guard magazine, he presented a proposal more similar to the eighteenth
century republican concept for the National Guard:

> In keeping with the traditional dual role of citizen-soldiers,
> the National Guard and Reserve can play a key part in maintaining a
> strong national defense and meeting important domestic needs. . . .
> To better meet post-Cold War threats, we should restructure our
> military forces away from defending against a short-warning, Soviet-
> style attack in Europe toward the mission of projecting forces to
> counter regional threats to U.S. interests. . . . Here too I have a
> fundamental disagreement with the [Bush] administration. It
> believes the Guard and Reserve forces should play a lesser role. I
> believe in a greater role for the Guard and Reserve in the aftermath
> of the Cold War. . . . The National Guard--through its citizen-
> soldiers--is an institution through which the American people are
> involved with the monumental decisions affecting war and peace. . .
> . The bottom line is that the National Guard is an effective
> military force for international and national missions. Its forces
> cost less than active duty troops, and it keeps our citizenry
> involved. . . . The Founding Fathers were right about the vital role
> of the citizen-soldier in our national security, and I would work to
> strengthen this role in the post-Cold War world.[31]

In this same issue appeared an article by Brian J. Boquist, a
reserve officer, who was highly critical of the Army's decision to
disband four National Guard light, motorized anti-armour Battalions.
Boquist accused the regular Army of having based this decision on
political grounds, and that it was motivated by the regular Army's

traditional animosity toward the Reserve forces. He sees the Cheney plan as part and parcel of a long standing conspiracy to marginalize the importance and contributions of the Reserve forces to the benefit of the professional military establishment:

> It could be stated the soldiers of the . . . [National Guard units] being deactivated . . . probably gave more to their country than their active counterparts. The citizen-soldiers who gave up their weekends to be trained, equipped, and prepared to serve their country also held civilian jobs to support their families and pay taxes during the week. Similar tax dollars have been over committed by the [Regular] military and government alike, thus creating a portion of the national debt to build a massive military industrial complex.

> This is a political rather than an economic issue. The Federal expenditures for the National Guard is 2.8 percent of the DoD's budget. To cut the National Guard in half will only save 1.4 percent of the budget. What would we be saving? We need to focus on realistic, future missions, not political and economic rhetoric.[32]

The tone of moral indignation present in Mr. Boquist article is equal to those passionate attacks on the regular military by "Brutus." and Senator Maclay would have been quick to endorse the allegations of conspiracy. This piece shows the depth of suspicion with which the proposals of the Regular establishment are still viewed by some Reservists. It also demonstrates the extent to which a claim to "superior" civic virtue is still an important ingredient in the debate on the relationship of the military to society.

The issue of deterrence is another important element in the preparedness discussion. An editorial in the November 26, 1991, edition of the Los Angeles Times, reflected decidedly Federalist notions about the pressure to significantly cut defense spending, then mounting

> There are far worse things that can be done to a defense budgets than load them up with yet more money to fund dubious programs. . . . Far worse would be to make spending cuts that would inevitably weaken the the military's ability to respond quickly to the kind of challenges that the coming years are most likely to bring. More than foolish, such an approach to budget cutting could well endanger national security.

126

As always, the budget, in the end a political document, will reflect tradeoffs and compromises. What the budget should not reflect is the kind of willful disregard of world political and security realities that characterized American military spending in the 1920 and '30s and that left us so initially unprepared for the war challenges of the early 1940s.[33]

A March 11, 1992, article by William Pfaff, in the same paper, expresses a traditionally republican criticism of a Defense Department draft proposal for a revised Bush administration national security strategy:

> The new Pentagon program for the the post-Cold War world . . . says that the United States policy should be to "convince" everyone else not to challenge "our leadership or seek . . . to overturn the established political and economic order. . . ." This Defense Department document obviously expresses the interests of the institution that produced it. It is a program to justify high military budgets and large military forces and national security bureaucracies for as long as the eye can see or the imagination stretch.
>
> . . . [the plan] disregards the fact that America's political leadership in the postwar years came from industrial and social accomplishment, and from the moral authority of dispassionate policy-making, rather than from simple military power. It is a plan for American world leadership through intimidation. It is a politically and morally stunted program whose logical outcome is to make the United States itself the . . . [threat] the Pentagon foresees. Is this what we want? To finish in a burlesque of empire?[34]

This view was seconded in a New Republic editorial appearing on 27 April 1992:

> The Bush administration has not yet explained why this country needs to remain a military superpower--indeed why it needs a strong defense at all. Its recently leaked Defense Planning Guidance, prepared by the Pentagon, offers little beyond the banal observation that the world remains a dangerous place and the odd looking bunch of possible [conflict] scenarios that have been taken apart by its critics.[35]

Among some modern conservatives the federalist anti-interventionist sentiments of Washington among others are also still active. Like Washington, these conservatives are in favor of maintaining a credible military deterent, but only for the sake of defending American territory proper, or, at most, clearly defined and tangible national interests. These conservatives keep alive the spirit of Washington's admonition in his farewell address to avoid "entangling foreign alliances." A prime example of this school of thought was provided by Patrick Buchanan in a Spring 1990 essay in The National Interest, entitled, "America First- and Second, and Third:"

> An island-continent, America should use her economic and technological superiority to keep herself permanent mistress of the seas, first in air power, first in space. . . . When defense cuts are made, they should come in army bases no longer needed for homeland defense, and ground troops no longer needed on foreign soil.
>
> We are not going to fight another land war in Asia; no vital interest justifies it; our people will not permit it. Why then keep another 30,000 ground troops on the [Korean] DMZ? . . . It is time we began uprooting the global network of "trip wires" planted on foreign soil to ensnare the United States in the wars of other nations, to back commitments made and treaties signed before this generation of American soldiers was born.[36]

A different, and more predominant conservative view of the deterence policy, however, appeared in a L.A. Times editorial in February 1992:

> Deterrence must remain the imperative when the United States assesses the prospect that a military-nationalist coup might one day restore Russia to a menacing international posture. That means maintaining sufficient strategic nuclear and ground forces to dissuade aggression, along with whatever other forces are deemed necessary to respond to regional conflicts.[37]

Attitudes Towards Governmental Military Power is the third of the criteria by which the similarities in the debate may be identified. The importance of maintaining a separation of authority over military power was a dominant issue in the eighteenth century. This issue still manifests itself in the continuing struggle between state and national authorities over primary control of the National Guard.

Despite successive acts of Congress from 1903 to 1952 subordinating state authority over the National Guard to the Federal Government, the 1980s witnessed repeated attempts by state governors to reassert control over state forces in defiance of federal directives. In 1985 and 1986, the governors of California and Maine attempted to block the deployment of state National Guard contingents to Honduras for annual training. In 1987, Massachusetts brought suit in federal court to reestablish the governor's authority to veto peacetime training deployments of National Guard units outside the state. These attempts were motivated by purely political opposition to President Reagan's Central American policies.[38] Though these vetoes were overturned by the courts, they provide an indication of the persistent political maneuvering occasioned by the Guard's dual status as state and federal troops.

Debate on the primacy of the state or Federal mission continues within the Guard itself. Samuel J. Newland, historian, and a member of the Kansas National Guard, viewed with alarm the governors' challenge to the Guard's national responsibilities:

> The National Guard exists today [1989], as it did in 1792, to defend the United States. Legally and historically, that is the chief rationale for its existence. Considering the experiences of the last century it seems unlikely that the states will expend the necessary funds to arm, equip, and train the National Guard to the level needed for a modern military force. Even were it willing, the nation can not be served effectively by a force trained and equipped according to the varied standards of 50 states. For the Governor of a state to veto training missions based on opposition to an administration's policies undermines the credibility of the national system.[39]

Major General (retired) Bruce Jacobs, historian for the National Guard association, would challenge Dr. Newland's assessment that the National Guard's primary identity is federal. While acknowledging the primacy of the federal reserve mission, he argues that: "under the law, and primarily, we are state troops."[40] Major General Jacobs sees state

service as the defining characteristic which sets Guard troops off from

other uniformed military personnel. He views discussion of immediate,

unsolicited, federal military intervention into local situations to

provide disaster relief, or to restore civil order as unnecessary, and

possibly ominous encroachments into traditional militia

responsibilities:

> We do not think history is on the side of those who would give
> the federal authorities a charter to dispatch rapid reaction forces
> before a request for help is made by a governor. We should never
> forget why, in 1878, the Congress, in its wisdom, passed the Posse
> Commitatus Act, placing limits on the use of federal military power
> at the local level.[41]

Beyond consideration of the relationship between the National

Guard and the Regular Army as separate components of military power, the

journals of the liberal movement continue to express high anxiety about

the purposes for which the Federal Government's uses its collective

military establishment. Reacting to the publication of a draft version

of the Defense Department's Defense Planning Guidance Memorandum 1994-

1999, an editorial in the May, 1992 edition of The Progressive entitled,

"Tomorrow the World." imputed sinister motives to the proposed defense

strategy:

> . . . If the national discourse had room for serious discussions of
> the most profound questions confronting us, then the dominant news
> of recent weeks would have been the Pentagon's draft [policy]. . . .
> What is most revealing about the document is its candor in outlining
> a U.S. foreign policy based on the determination to sustain world
> domination by relying on military force. . . . [foreign diplomats]
> were "sharply critical of some of the language in the document."
> They had good reason to be. Rife with references to economic
> rivalries and trade competition, the report implies that such
> conflicts will ultimately be settled by U.S. resort to military
> means. It is the Pentagon's bid to become the final arbiter of this
> country's economic and political role in the world, not just its
> military posture.[42]

In January 1992, Rolling Stone dedicated its "National Affairs"
column to a William Greider article in which he condemns the "political
conspiracy" he saw behind the continued funding of the defense budget:

> Perhaps you've seen the news on TV that the Soviet Union has
> disintegrated. Or you've read something in the papers about huge
> cuts proposed for the U.S. defense budget. Maybe you assumed that
> after forty years of costly struggle with communism, the United
> States could at last get on with the business of peace and
> prosperity at home. Maybe you thought the Cold War was over. You
> were wrong.

> The enemy may have vanished, but the political engine that
> powered the cold-war era extravaganza for four decades is still
> very much in place and chugging purposefully forward. The members
> of the military-industrial complex, along with their frontmen and
> apologists in government and the media, have no intention of
> retiring gracefully. Instead, they're busy devising new "threats"
> to scare Americans into tolerating a bloated defense budget.[43]

In a March 9, 1992 opinion piece in The Nation, Robert L.
Borosage seconded Greider's analysis. Borosage claimed that: "Half the
U.S. military budget--about $150 billion a year--has been devoted to
defending Europe and Japan against a threat that no longer exists."[44]
He accused President Bush of deliberately obfuscating the rational
behind the 1993 defense budget: "The President, reared on the cold war,
has a simple 'mission.' He will defend as much of the military budget as
he can."[45] Borosage sounded this theme again in a May 11 editorial.
Expressing outrage over the passage of the Administrations defense
budget, he unfavorably compared this action with what he regarded as the
country's appropriate historical response to the end of a conflict:

> The country has once again been mugged in the halls of Congress.
> On March 31 the House of Representatives voted 238 to 187 against
> transferring even a nickel from the military to domestic programs.
> . . . Contrast this with the end of World War II. Military spending
> was reduced by 90 percent in three years. More than 21 million
> Americans transferred from wartime to peacetime employment. The
> G.I. Bill helped millions with stipends for education and training,
> and loans for houses.

> . . . Truman initially wanted to maintain a large military in
> garrisons around the world. Congress probably would have gone

along, but it was buried under a deluge of baby shoes sent in by
mothers demanding that absent fathers be brought home. If we are
ever to reap any benefit from the end of the cold war, there must be
a similar independent mobilization, with citizens calling their
representatives to their senses.[46]

In a September 15, 1992 speech to the National Guard
association, President Bush defended his budget using arguments that
directly parallel the traditional federalist attitudes towards military
preparedness:

> . . . The fact is: For all the great gains we've made for freedom,
> for all the peace of mind we've secured for the young people in this
> country, the world remains a dangerous place. The Soviet Bear may
> be extinct, but there are still plenty of wolves in the world;
> dictators with missiles, narco-terrorists trying to take over whole
> countries, ethnic wars, regional flashpoints, madmen we can't allow
> to get a finger on the nuclear trigger.
>
> . . . Our task is to guard against the crises that haven't caught
> fire, the wars that are waiting to happen, the threats that will
> come with little or no warning. I make this promise: As long as I
> am President, our services will remain the best trained, the best
> equipped, the best led fighting forces in the world. This is the
> way we guarantee the peace.[47]

The Clinton administration too, has failed to escape
ideologically motivated criticism of the administration's continuing
level of defense preparedness. Following the "Bottom-up" review
directed by the new Defense Secretary, Les Aspin, liberal critics were
quick to take exception to the proposed defense reductions and
realignments as being too conservative. A September 1993 letter to the
Washington Post by Carl Conetta and Charles Knight underscored this
position:

> Contrary to the suggestion [by the Washington post Editors] that
> the Clinton administration's bottom-up review of future defense
> requirements is "about right," the review inflates potential
> military threats and proposes extravagant ways of dealing with them.
> The result is a proposed military force and budget that is at least
> one-quarter larger than America will need during the next 10-15
> years.
>
> This approach [cutting defense by an additional 25 percent] may
> entail some added risk. Wining two wars at the same time, should

132

this ever be necessary, would likely take a few extra weeks, but
measured against the benefits of redistributing $40 billion to $50
billion per year to economic revival, this small risk seems worth
taking.[48]

An editorial appearing in National Review in March 1993, was
equally, however oppositely, critical that the new Administration was
dangerously eroding the country's defenses on the basis of purely
political considerations:

> Last week, the Clinton Administration decreed a $11 billion cut
> in the last Bush defense budget, or a cut of more than 3.5 percent.
> How was the slice administered? The services were told to figure
> out (over the weekend) ways of cutting about $2.5 billion each, plus
> an Initiative. Not much strategic calculation here. . . . The
> fault lies not with Mr. Aspin, but with an Administration that has,
> with breathtaking speed, made it clear that it knows little, and
> cares less about sound defense policy." It began its term subverting
> the cohesion of the armed forces through its efforts to lift the ban
> on homosexuals in the services; it has effectively designated the
> Pentagon as a quick cash machine to cover domestic expenditure. . .
> .[49]

The hostility expressed by the National Review to Clinton's
ambition to expand the demographic base of the military by increasing
the participation of historically excluded groups, is a manifestation of
another historic area of friction. The issue of balanced class
representation in the military is encompassed by the 2nd criteria for
comparison; the contrast between the republican versus federalist
concept of the relationship of the military to society. As previously
noted, it was a fundamental tenant of 1790s republicanism that, to be
legitimate, the military must be representative of the society as a
whole. This argument is used with increasing frequency in the 1990s as
a justification for the repeal of the ban on homosexuals in military
service, and for the inclusion of women in military combat roles. The
issue of representation was raised by Yale Law professor, Paul W. Kahn
in a March 1993 article for The New Republic:

> Perhaps a more representative military will actually serve as a
> counterforce to the increasing tendency to view military life as

133

merely a form of employment. . . . What is the realistic form of the military in the twenty-first century? Will military service be so changed by modern technology and modern ideas of the liberal state in a world community, that it will simply become another form of employment through which individuals maintain their private families? Much of the military has already reached this point. Surely Clinton is right to see the vast unfairness in excluding any qualified individual from these opportunities.[50]

In addition to a concern with maintaining a balanced social representation, republican ideology was deeply mistrustful of the anti-democratic influence of rigid military discipline. This theme continues to be sounded by those who object to the curtailment of civil liberties inherent in regular military service. In a New Republic article objecting to the criminalization of homosexuality in the military, and the methods used to enforce these regulations, contributing editor Scott Shuger claimed that:

> The enforcement of the ban is invariably cruel, brutal, and without virtually any of the legal safeguards civilians take for granted in judicial proceedings. In a culture populated mostly by the young and legally unsophisticated, policed by investigators with wide ranging powers of seizure and detention, and controlled by commanders with tremendous discretionary power, the ban fosters an inquisitional climate much worse than civilians can imagine.[51]

Republicanism concerned itself first and foremost with the rights of the individual. In similar fashion, the arguments for the inclusion of gays and women are grounded primarily on the notion that exclusion from service is a violation of basic individual civil rights. Just as in the 1790s, the modern liberals apprehensions over these issues reflects a bias that is societal rather than institutional. These Democrats are not concerned with the effect of changed policies on the military services, but essentially with using the services as a means of forwarding their social and political agendas. David R. Carlin, Jr., eloquently stated this observation in a January 1993 article in the Commonweal:

> Now, the gay rights movement is inspired by an individualist mentality, not a spirit of institutionalism; in fact it is probably

the most striking example on the current American scene of the philosophy of radical individualism. Those pushing for admission of homosexuals to the military are not doing so because they have a profound personal commitment to the well-being of Army, Navy, and Air Force; they could care less about these institutions. They are doing so because they have a profound personal commitment to promoting and defending what they conceive to be the rights of gays and lesbians.[52]

The old Federalist institutional paradigms are also very much alive. Just as were Henry Knox and Alexander Hamilton, the majority of conservative commentators are interested, primarily, that the military remain capable of accomplishing its wartime missions, and are unconcerned with any demographic lopsidedness, or gender and orientational inequalities. In response to what he termed "the Feminist assault on the military," author David Horowitz made the following assertion in the October 1992 edition of National Review:

> It is hardly necessary to have the detailed information that the military has decided to suppress, to see that America's ability to wage war has been weakened by the deployment of relatively large numbers of women to an overseas battle-field, even absent a combat role. Who does not remember the poignant stories the networks did in lavish detail about the children left behind by their mothers dispatched to war duty in the Persian Gulf? . . . Now, the purpose an mission of the American military are held to be of less concern than the need to eradicate any possible injustice that might be associated with the exclusion of women. . . .[53]

In another section of the same article, Horowitz quoted testimony delivered before the Presidential Commission on the Assignment of women in the Armed Forces as an example of the ulterior liberal motives behind this issue suspected by many conservatives:

> Maria Lepowski, a professor of Womens Studies, provided the commissioners with data to support a combat role for women. Then Professor Lepowski asked herself: "What would be some possible consequences [of women in combat roles]--on American cultural values and American society. . . ?" She answered her own question: "I think there might be increased concern about committing troops to combat, also perhaps a good thing. . . ." In other words, Professor Lepowsky was advocating that women be put in combat roles because to do so would make it more difficult to commit troops to combat. Now this is a kind of candor that is unusual on the left.[54]

135

This overriding concern with efficiency is also apparent in the objections voiced to the termination of the military ban on homosexuals. E.L Pattullo, former director of the Center for Behavioral Sciences at Harvard University, was frank in voicing this opinion in the March 1993, edition of National Review:

> The American military is highly responsive to civilian control, and it is thoroughly professional. If ordered to do so it will find ways to adapt to the enlistment of individuals who proudly declare themselves gay. But doing so has the potential to diminish permanently the efficiency of combat troops. Is the gain for the gay community worth the likely loss in the effectiveness of our military? . . . Thanks to their professionalism our armed forces will survive, but they will be weakened. Though hard to quantify, the cost to morale will be real and lasting.[55]

These concerns with military effectiveness raise the specter of a return to the "hollow force" of the 1970s. On paper, the American military forces of the Ford and Carter eras showed formidable strength in men and materiel. Due to sparse funding, however, units were undermanned, poorly trained, and equipment was badly maintained. In light of accelerating budget cutbacks, many analysts see a return of this situation as immanent. Reporter Art Pine noted these sentiments in a June 1993 story for the Los Angeles Times:

> . . . Visions of the 1970s are returning as the military's rapidly shrinking budget begins to sap funds for training, maintenance, and recruiting, which are essential for readiness. . . . [furthermore] the military is facing myriad social changes that some analysts fear could spawn morale problems and ultimately affect readiness as well. Service personnel already are worried about the impact of the military cutbacks on their own futures. But the armed forces also are expanding the role of women in combat posts and most likely will ease the current ban on homosexuals. All represent changes--and adjustments--from the traditional military ways. . . . [But] the going won't be easy. Unless [Secretary of Defense] Aspin and the Administration can deliver on every single promise they made, they will confront a hollow military whether they like it or not. . . .[56]

Inevitably, those alarmed by the specter of a hollow force have critics of a more traditionally republican bent. Advocates of still greater defense budget cuts usually disregard the fears of more

conservative colleagues by accusing the advocates of large defense
spending of having their own ulterior personal, political, and economic
motives. This attitude is exemplified by a John Isaacs article
appearing in The Bulletin of Atomic Scientists in the July/August 1993
issue:

> . . . [During House Appropriation Committee debate on a defense
> budget increase of $1.2 billion, Chairman John Murtha] predicted a
> return to the days of Jimmy Carter's so-called "hollow army," which
> he said was not properly trained or prepared to fight. "That means
> that accident rates will increase and the quality of life for the
> military will be reduced. . . . Members were not always clear or to
> the point when justifying the new spending. Cong. Joseph McDade
> contended that eliminating the 1.2 billion would "begin to step back
> toward the hollow Army, hollow Navy, the hollow Marine Corps" of the
> late 1970s. But he never quite explained the connection between
> executive jets [one designated use of the money] and "crippled"
> armed forces. . . . In a moment of candor . . . Murtha conceded his
> true motivation. While the Pentagon preferred to cut various
> programs, "We felt they were taking out members programs and
> [changing] priorities we were interested in." In other words, he
> wanted to protect the pork he and other members coveted for their
> own districts.[57]

During the Administration of Thomas Jefferson, one justification
for the expense involved in maintaining a comparatively large standing
army was to use them for a variety of peacetime government functions.
In the days of the early republic, these activities included serving as
a police force for the federal frontier territories, exploration and
surveying of new lands, road construction and other civil-engineering
projects.[58] These activities are mirrored today by the rapidly
expanding sphere of non-combat roles and missions being assumed by the
Department of Defense. The Army is attempting to assimilate these new
roles by integrating them into its basic operational doctrine.

The June 1993 edition of Field Manual 100-5, "Operations"--the
Army's cap-stone "how to" manual for military operations--elevates these
non-combat missions, or "Operations Other Than War" in the current
argot, to a status nearly equal with more traditional military

activities.[59] FM 100-5 identifies some of these activities as:
"Support to Domestic Civil Authorities, Humanitarian Assistance and
Disaster Relief, and "Support to Counter Drug Operations."[60] The
military's success and effectiveness in these areas, such as: disaster
relief efforts after major Hurricanes in Hawaii and Florida in 1992, The
National Guard and regular Army assistance in restoring order to riot
torn Los Angeles the same year, and the aid to drug interdiction efforts
on-going since the mid-1980s, have led to increasing suggestions from
many quarters to expand the military's involvement in solving a broad
spectrum of domestic problems.

This inclination was dramatically highlighted in October 1993
when Washington, D.C., Mayor Sharon Pratt Kelly formally requested that
the President authorize the use of local National Guard troops (under
permanent Federal control due to Washington's unique status as a Federal
district) to help the police in routine law enforcement operations.[61]
Mayor Kelly's request met with a storm of protest from across the
political spectrum, but Democratic arguments tended to center on the
republican objection to the potential for increased Federal infringement
on civil liberties.

A similar, though less widely publicized debate occurred in
California in November 1993, when the Editors of the Los Angeles Times
suggested that the National Guard be used to supplement the efforts of
the U.S. Border Patrol along the Mexican-U.S. border. The Times
reasoned that protecting the economy of the South-West from inundation
by low wage illegal immigrants was a natural, and economical, extension
of the Guard's responsibility to protect the nation from external
threat.[62]

This suggestion met with a vehement objection from California
Representative Barbara Boxer, who viewed it as an unacceptable

138

militarization of domestic law enforcement, and equated such methods with fascism.[63] Other doubts about the morality and democratic propriety of using the military to help enforce domestic order were forwarded by Joseph D. McNamara in a _L.A. Times_ column titled: "Police vs. National Guard: can you protect and serve and kill the enemy?"[64] These arguments reflect both the extent to which republican anxiety about domestic military power still influences public discourse, and the degree to which increasing federal control of the National Guard has eroded that institution's republican legitimacy in the eyes of extreme liberals.

Conservative resistance to this multiplication of military missions is grounded, along with so many of the arguments just enumerated, in that federalist fixation on pure military effectiveness. These critics see the expansion of military roles, foreign and domestic, as also serving liberal goals of rendering the military democratically acceptable by converting it into a comparatively harmless engine of social change—a kind of armed adjunct to the Peace Corps. Military commentator Harry Summers expressed this fear in a column entitled: "And Don't Forget That Armies Are, Primarily, for Fighting Wars."[65] In this piece, Summers is critical of those who sarcastically accuse the senior Defense Department leadership of being too reluctant and cautious to commit U.S. Forces to domestic and international peacekeeping and humanitarian efforts. To make his point, Summers quotes remarks by General Colin Powell on the subject:

> Powell and the other senior members of the joint chiefs . . . know what military forces are for: "Not withstanding all the changes that have taken place in the world, notwithstanding the new emphasis on peace-keeping, peace enforcement, peace engagement, preventative diplomacy, we have a value system and a culture system within the armed forces of the United States," Powell said earlier this month. "We have this mission: to fight and win the nation's wars. . . ."

"Because we are warriors, we are also uniquely able to do some of these new other missions that are coming along . . . . But we never want to do it in such a way that we lose sight of the focus of why you have armed forces--to fight and win the nation's wars.[66]

In order to cope with these new missions expectations, Colonel Charles E. Heller, Ph.D., Reserve Forces Advisor to the U.S. Army War College's Strategic Studies Institute, himself an active-duty reservist, has proposed, in essence, the adoption of a slightly modified version of the "Peace Establishment" plan first proposed by Alexander Hamilton in 1783. In his work, Twenty-First Century Force: A Federal Army And A Militia, published in 1993, Heller made the following historical analysis of the Army's failure to maintain a consistently battle worthy force during the 20th century:

The Army has consistently underestimated the political clout of the National Guard as exercised through two organizations, The Adjutant General Association (AGA) and the National Guard Association of the United States (NGAUS), and, as a consequence, has had difficulty in structuring a peacetime force.

The Army has a very poor institutional memory, and while creating a more responsive Federal Reserve force in the 20th century has consistently forgotten why it did so in the first place. While at times the Reserve Officers Association (ROA) has lobbied as effectively as the Guard's Association's, its membership is smaller and is reluctant to publicly challenge the Active Component leadership.

The Army has consistently failed to understand the traditional American reluctance to maintain sufficient Regular Army forces in Peace-time to meet future opponents. It also fails to remember that, throughout most of its history, it has engaged in domestic missions more often than wars.[67]

From these and related analyses, Heller draws the conclusion that: "a restructuring of the Total Army must take place for it to meet the national security and domestic challenges in the 21st century." [68] Heller would reorganize these forces into two components; a Federal Army consisting of the Active Army and the U.S. Army Reserve, and a militia composed of the state Army National Guard. Under this concept the focus of the active component would be to maintain forward presence, and perform contingency missions with the support of the Federal Reserve operating under the same laws and standards in peace and war.

The role of the National Guard would be returned to that of the late 18th century. Heller's primary focus for the Guard would be to support the state missions as assigned by the governors. He contends that this would eliminate the problem of attempting to train for two diverse and separate missions (state and federal) with insufficient time to justice to either. Heller cites as evidence of this problem certain National Guard roundout brigades' alleged inability to deploy quickly during the Persian Gulf Crisis and problems that arose during the L.A. riot.[69]

He believes that the by terminating the Guards roundout and early deployment missions, the necessary time would be created for training and reorganization that would allow the Guard to be effectively used for reinforcement and reconstitution of the Federal Army in a major conflict. Heller believes that: "This structure returns the roles and missions of each component to its Constitutional authority," and "reflects the strengths of each component, the American military tradition and the reality of a peacetime force in a constrained budget environment."[70]

Heller's assessment of the readiness problems facing the Reserve forces, if not his recommendation to adopt the old federalist proposals, have been seconded by many other analysts. In their study of the issue, Martin Binkin and William W. Kaufman of the Brookings Institution also identified many of the readiness problems that continue to beset the Total Force concept.[71] Chief among these, they found, was the influence of partisan and ideologically motivated politics on defense policy debate:

141

The Total Force policy may have its detractors, but few can be found in Congress. On the contrary, the reserves have long benefited from pressure exerted on their behalf by legislators influenced by broad grass roots support and a strong, well organized lobby. The network of reserve units has been described as a part of the "intricate and subtle political chain that laces the country, running through village council rooms, county court houses, and state capitals to Congress and the White House."[72]

Major General Bruce Jacobs was also candid in his assessment of the role of politics in Guard Policy. "There is still," he says, "a very heavy political component [in Guard legislation]. The Guard had demeaning experiences in Vietnam and the Persian Gulf and will not now, willingly, write itself out of the Army's warplans." If it were to do so, Jacobs believes it "would have very real [negative] consequences for Guard morale."[73] The Guard also remains very aware that the Regular Army has an historical record of neglecting the Guard unless forced by Congressional mandate or circumstances to supply it with adequate resources and training opportunities.[74]

The current Democratic Administration remains as committed to the Total Force policy as were the Republican--Democrats of the 18th century to the militia. In the September 1993 edition of the Reserve Officers Association National Security Report, Assistant Secretary of Defense for Reserve Affairs Deborah R. Lee wrote:

It has been my observation that the Reserves in each service are committed to excellence, and continually seek innovative ways to improve the readiness of our forces. In this twentieth anniversary year of the Total Force policy, the "Total Force" is no longer a concept, but a reality, and stronger than ever. We have an impressive team, great leadership, and I am confident we will enjoy much success as we face the challenges in the future. . . . The new force structure will certainly require that we rely more heavily on the Reserve components. This is because the Reserve Forces are cost effective and are adapting to the challenges that the future presents.[75]

The senior professional military leadership recognizes this commitment and adapts its own policies and programs to conform with the sentiments of the civil authorities. Army Chief of Staff General Gordon R. Sullivan is careful to refer to the Army in public statements as "America's Army" (emphasis in the original).[76] This reflects both a desire to demonstrate the regular Army's commitment to the Total Force policy, and, perhaps, an ongoing concern that the professional military not become politically or socially isolated from the mass of the country.

This concern to prevent military isolation is also demonstrated in the remarks presented to the 1993/94 class of the U.S. Army Command and General Staff College by General Bruce Reimer, Commander, United States Forces Command, in January 1994. On a presentation slide listing the "Roles of Forces Command," Reimer included: "Maintain contact with American Society."[77] Referring to this slide entry, Gen Reimer commented: "This is a major contribution of the Guard and Reserve forces. The local armories help keep us [American society and the military] together politically and socially."[78] This is an assessment that echoes the sentiments held by both George Washington and Thomas Jefferson.

Reimer went on to comment on the current American defense situation in terms that, save for the change in jargon over the intervening centuries, could have summed up America's defense posture in 1796:

> The Army is no longer capable of going to war without the Reserve Component. Therefore, Reserve Component readiness is now a critical requirement for Forces Command. The selective service system is terminated and resources are coming down--realistically, [combat] replacements over the short term are going to come from the Reserve Components.[79]

The April 1993 edition of Parameters, the quarterly journal of the Army War College, carried a fictional story by U.S. Air Force Lieutenant Colonel Charles Dunlap, Jr., entitled, "The Origins of the

American Military Coup in 2012."[80] Dunlap's story is written from the perspective of a senior military officer courtmartialed and sentenced to be executed for attempting to oppose the take-over. On the eve of his execution, the officer smuggles a letter out of prison in which he traces the events that led up to the Coup. He states that the military's infringement on public authority was: "the outgrowth of trends visible as far back as 1992" and included "the massive diversion of military forces to civilian uses."[81] Trading on the military's high level of public trust after the Gulf War, the politicians enlisted the armed forces into an ever expanding array of non-military activities.

Armed troops became adjuncts to, first national, and then local police agencies. Redundant military bases became prisons and drug rehab centers. Military medical units were used to treat poor and indigent civilians. Military engineers were recruited to repair public housing, rebuild highways and bridges, and manage toxic waste (all of which represent real political proposals made between 1991 and 92). Dunlap speculates that by the year 2000: "the armed forces had penetrated many vital aspects of American society." The politicians made, "a terrible mistake which allowed the armed forces to be diverted from their original purpose . . . to support and defend the government, not to _be_ the government."[82]

The story continues, that in order to efficiently execute these myriad missions, the military began to demand an increasing role in policy making decisions. When the President suddenly died in 2012, the senior generals simply took control. With the military already so deeply embedded in national domestic life, this seemed not only acceptable to most people, but even natural.

This apocryphal tale struck a cord at both ends of the political spectrum. In the difference between the conservative and liberal interpretation of the story, the fundamental differences in political ideologies are apparent. Conservative Harry Summers concluded that in the atmosphere of social engineering and extra-military operations that supplanted the traditional warrior ethic: "it is little wonder that its [the military's] traditional apolitical professionalism eroded. Hence the coup. We ignore his [Dunlap's] cautionary tale at our peril."[83]

Writing in The Nation, columnist David Corn gave the story a republican slant: "Dunlap's point is one ignored in public discussion: The military should be a limited force. Skepticism toward organized state power is a healthy American tradition."[84] Both interpretations eloquently demonstrate the continuing influence of traditional republican and federalist ideology in American defense policy debates.

Historian Richard Kohn has taken a less extreme view than Dunlap of the current trends in American civil-military relations, but it is no less a traditional one. In an April 11th piece for the New York Times, entitled; "Upstarts in Uniform," Dr. Kohn opined that the Cold War had effected dangerous changes in the attitudes of the professional military and that it had come to see itself as: "separate in society, with its own needs and interests--adept at using the media, maneuvering inside the bureaucracy . . . and increasingly pronouncing publicly on issues of war, peace and policy."[85] Dr. Kohn goes on to suggest that the military should withdraw into "personal and professional neutrality abandoning participation in public debate about foreign and military policy." Kohn concluded his piece with a sentiment that exactly mirrors traditional republican concern with the influence of a standing military: "The Republic is not in immediate danger. But a consciously separate military participating actively in policy and national debate can only erode democracy."[86]

CHAPTER 7

CONCLUSION

In its handling of the problem of civilian control of the armed forces, the United States, in this as in so many other political mechanisms, has clung to archaic methods easily explicable in terms of American history, less easily defended in terms of efficiency or safety in our dangerous world, so unlike that contemplated by the "Founding Fathers" in 1787.[1]

This judgment by historian Michael Howard neatly delineates the challenge faced by anyone wishing to impose significant reform on the basic structures of the United States military establishment. The separation of powers, and especially the division of military responsibility inherent in the U.S. Constitution reflects the twin hopes and fears of America's early leaders. They hoped to provide real security against any foreign or domestic threat. They feared that any force capable of providing such security would itself become the engine of freedom's destruction.

The dilemma facing American Government was how to maintain a level of military efficiency sufficient to deter or defeat aggressors, while simultaneously protecting the people's liberties from the military's potential ambitions. The disparate solutions to this dilemma favored by republicans or nationalists naturally reflected their ideological prejudices against one, or the other risk. Republican ideology inclined its adherents to fear a centralization of military power in the national government more than any external foreign threat. Nationalists, conversely, believed that a weak central government, and reliance on citizen militias were an open invitation to external aggression and encouraged internal rebellion and anarchy. The

146

constitutional compromises needed to reconcile these divergent positions necessarily reflected the ideological tensions inherent in the republican - nationalist dichotomy.

Liberalism has dominated American political thinking since the earliest colonial period.[2] Even those major factions in American politics such as big business who are called, for the want of a more precise term, "Conservatives," are, by the standards of political philosophy, or the political practice of much of the world, liberal. The concepts of a freemarket and laissez-faire economics, themselves the child of that quintessential Enlightenment philosopher Adam Smith, are liberal to their core.

Initially, liberalism was the intellectual legacy of the first European colonists. The continuing dominance of liberalism, however, was a result not of inheritance, but of the isolation, social homogeneity, and unique historical experiences of the American people. In light of this fact, political historian Samuel P. Huntington has asserted that; "in the absence of European feudalism, European classes, and a European proletariat, political struggle in America was restricted to squabbles for limited objectives among interest groups all of whom shared the same basic values."[3]

Huntington cited these, "amorphous goals and values," as collectively comprising an American "Creed."[4] The central, constant values of the American Creed stemmed from different aspects of the American philosophical and political experience, but they represent nonetheless closely related ideas. Broadly, these values are; " liberty, equality, individualism, democracy, and the rule of law under a constitution."[5] These values are by no means the exclusive property of the American people, but, due to the unique circumstances of

American history they had a more profound impact upon it than most other societies. As Huntington points out:

> In America, ideology in the form of the principles of the American Creed existed before the formation of a national community and political system. These principles defined the identity of the community when there were no institutions for dealing with the other countries of the world.[6]

At the beginning of the Revolution, most American leaders assumed that such institutions as would be required to fulfill the domestic and international functions of government would naturally reflect this underlying ideology. The functional imperatives of such governmental institutions are, however, antithetical to the liberal-democratic values of the American Creed. Governmental institutions must be strong to be effective, but strong executive, military, intelligence, and police agencies are, by their very nature authoritarian and hierarchical. The essence of the Creed is opposition to precisely such power and concentrated authority.[7]

The intrinsic conflict between the ideals of the American Creed and the practical requirements of conducting military operations or of instilling order with in civil society created the schism in American liberal philosophy that eventually resulted in the formation of separate Republican-Democrat and Federalist parties. These organizations shared the same goal; an independent union of American states whose government reflected the closest possible approximation of the values expressed in the American Creed. They differed fundamentally, however, in their vision of how this goal was to be achieved.

Naturally, the complex set of political values, ideological influences, and moral convictions held by any one individual defy simple summation. Among the Founding Fathers, political opinion spanned a continuum from the dogmatically republican Elbridge Gerry to the elitist Alexander Hamilton. Furthermore, a person's political convictions are subject to change over time. For this reason staunch nationalist James Madison became, by the middle 1790s, a key member of Jefferson's republican inner circle. Likewise, republican firebrand Patrick Henry died a Federalist. Nevertheless, an individual's primary association with one or the other group will generally indicate his adherence to the basic republican or federalist ideas identified by the criteria established in Chapter Three:

1. Attitude Towards Government Power:

Republicanism's attitude towards centralized government power was essentially hostile. Republicans preferred a loose association of states and a broad distribution of political and administrative power. They believed that a powerful central government would inevitably usurp the prerogatives of the states and extend its authority despotically over all aspects of private life. They subscribed to a vaguely defined theory of mankind's "natural" virtue, and trusted that in the absence of strong central directing authority, a selfless, patriotic commitment to republicanism would provide that spirit of cooperation necessary for unified action. They believed that a decentralized, highly democratized military establishment was they only type of organization that was both safe and compatible with the American Creed's basic values.

Federalism concerned itself more with external threats. Federalists regarded a strong central government as a prerequisite for the maintenance of that security and domestic tranquility necessary for the fulfillment of meaningful liberty. They relied upon the limitations and separations of power provided for in the Constitution to provide the necessary protection from autocratic ambition. Federalists took a cynical view of man's essential character. Federalists expected Americans to exhibit, in the same proportion, that

venality and self-interest which had bedeviled all recorded societies.
They favored a mechanistic approach to these problems, and believed
that the darker tendencies of both individuals and institutions could
be canceled out by setting the competing interests against each other
in a system of checks and balances. Provided the proper balances were
in place, Federalists saw no extraordinary inherent danger in a
professional military.

2. Attitude Towards the Relationship Between the Military and
Society:

Republicanism held that to be legitimate, the military must be
representative of the broader society from which it springs.
Republicans regarded service in the militia as a fundamental civic
responsibility, and took the extent to which this obligation was
honored as one measure of the public virtue which they so highly
esteemed. They were contemptuous and suspicious of paid regular troops
and regarded them as essentially mercenary. They were concerned lest
an over reliance upon such troops foster decadence by encouraging
citizens to shirk their responsibilities.

Republicans were especially suspicious of the motives of
regular army officers. The officers detachment from the surrounding
local and regional communities led some to question their loyalty and
political reliability. These concerns aside, republicans of a populist
bent resented the undemocratic detachment and "airs" in the military
bearing of regular officers. Some republicans regarded the
professional military as a would-be privileged class who wanted to loaf
through life at public expense.

Federalism primarily concerned itself that the military
establishment be capable of providing effective defense. Federalists'
practical experiences with traditional militia had given them a low
opinion of citizen soldiers. They regarded ideological enthusiasm as

150

dangerously fickle, and a poor substitute for conventional drill and discipline. Furthermore, they were suspicious of the local political entanglements of the militia officers. Federalists regarded the parochial outlook and nepotism common among the militia as compromising the militia officers performance of military duties.

Federalists did not care whether the members of the regular military establishment were fully representative of their society. In fact, they expected that regular soldiers would not be representative since the low pay and relative lack of prestige of soldiers tended to favor recruitment from the lower economic classes. Federalists intended that the small number, strict discipline, and apolitical nature of regular troops would mitigate any potential domestic threat posed by them.

3. Attitude Towards Military Preparedness:

Republicanism regarded a high constant state of military preparedness as a dangerous temptation to internal repression, and external foreign adventure. They resented significant expenditures of money in the absence of a tangible, immediate threat. They viewed the maintenance of regular standing forces in the name of deterrence as redundant to the function of the militia. A fundamental republican tenant was that a free, armed, and patriotic citizenry was the best guarantor of liberty. They therefore regarded the alleged justifications for standing professional forces as being primarily motivated by the military's desire to further its own institutional interests.

Federalism accepted a high level of military preparedness as being the most effective deterrent to conflict. They rejected republican claims that the traditional militia could, without fundamental restructuring, achieve and maintain competent levels of combat readiness. Federalists believed that military skills are highly perishable and require constant exercise. They considered consistent investment in the maintenance of these skills to be a superior financial and moral economy to crash programs begun only in the face of imminent hostilities. They did not, however, view the possession of strong military forces as promoting an American interventionist policy in foreign affairs. Indeed they hoped that the maintenance of a strong military deterence would secure freedom from the necessity to seek foreign military alliances.

Federalism dominated American politics from the mid 1780s through the 1790s. After 1800, however, federalism was rapidly eclipsed by a resurgent Jeffersonian republicanism. Subsequent American history demonstrated that the ideological concerns of both these political movements were valid. Federalism's assessment of the inadequacies of the traditional militia system was proven accurate, with tragic consequences, during the War of 1812. Republican President James Madison's misplaced reliance on militia, and Congress' penurious refusal to raise adequate regular forces resulted in unmitigated military disaster for the United States. Only the unpopularity of the war in Britain, and the half-hearted prosecution of the American campaigns by the British Military due to the strain of the Napoleonic Wars prevented the American defeats from fundamentally effecting the course of U.S. development.

Furthermore, the republican administrations of Jefferson, Madison, and James Monroe all found it expedient, once in power, to retain most of the Federalist innovations introduced by the hated Hamilton. Despite their bitter opposition to standing armies, these presidents not only continued the existence of the permanent establishment, but strengthened it. Because of continuing threats along the western frontier, Jefferson added additional regular garrisons in the central and southern sections. To help relieve the

152

chronic shortage of engineers, Jefferson and Madison created the
military academy first proposed by Washington, and completed the other
non-militia portions of the original peace establishment plan as well.

For good or ill, many of the more dire republican predictions
about centralized government power have, over the intervening two
hundred years, also come to fruition. A preference for regular troops
and federal volunteers after the War of 1812 did cause the militia
system to wither into irrelevancy until its partial revival as the
National Guard. During the U.S. Civil War, Federal troops invaded
thirteen southern states attempting to secede from the Union and forced
their capitulation at bayonet point.

Most tellingly, the Federal Armed Forces have been repeatedly
used on active military campaigns within and without the territorial
United States on the sole authority of the Executive. Indeed, no U.S.
president has yet admitted any constitutional congressional power to
limit the Executive's authority to commit the Armed Forces to battle.
Since the ratification of the Constitution through the present, Federal
authority has gained steadily at the expense of state and local
autonomy. Today there is scarcely any aspect of private life not
influenced directly by the federal power.

Early in the 19th century federalism collapsed as a coherent
political movement, and traditional Jeffersonian republicanism began to
be supplanted by Jacksonian populism. Since, however, republicanism
and federalism were competing ideological factions within the broader
framework of American liberalism, many of their basic tenants,
including the military ones, survived the demise of their parent
philosophies. Detached from their original context, they became free
to be recombined in new patterns, and have been absorbed by more recent
political movements. In so far as these ideological threads have
become inextricably bound up with the basic values of the American

153

Creed, they will continue to survive and influence public attitudes towards the military.

The persistent influence of these ideologies on the modern defense debate, and their parallels to the 18th century debate were demonstrated in Chapter five. Naturally, allowance must be made for the changes in reference and circumstances over two centuries, but the influences of the (slightly modified) historical ideologies are nonetheless discernible. The parallels in the two periods are most clearly observable by dividing modern adherents to modified forms of republicanism or federalism into somewhat simplistic categories of "liberals" and "conservatives."

The terms liberal and conservative most closely approximate in tone and meaning the old 18th century labels, and are commonly used to imply an affiliation with the left (Liberal), or right (Conservative), ends of the political spectrum just as were republican and federalist in their day. By then applying to these categories the criteria developed in Chapter three, the historical parallels and the continuing influence of the ideologies become readily apparent:

1. Attitudes Towards Government Military Power:

Modern liberals retain the traditional republican mistrust and suspicion of military power. They regard the regular military establishment as primarily concerned with expanding its own power and influence. Many believe that the military manufactures, or wildly exaggerates the potential military threats to the nation in order to maintain or increase the force structure, and to secure backing for unnecessary weapons procurement. They further believe that the existence of such excessive military power provides an often irresistible temptation to settle international disputes through the application of armed force. They tend to believe that the military favors an early resort to force in most international situations in order to justify its own existence.

In order to counteract these trends, liberals favor an increased reliance on National Guard and Reserve forces because of their perception that reliance upon such forces imposes an additional level of military restraint due to the political costs associated with mobilizing reserves and disrupting local economies. They also regard the reserve forces as preferable to the regular military due to its perception as a primarily civilian oriented organization. Liberals are as unsympathetic with the professional military's authoritarianism and military ethic as were their 18th century counterparts, and they seek ways in which the military can be rendered more democratic. They are skeptical of military objections that such democratization is incompatible with military efficiency and often regard such arguments as evasive or reactionary.

A significant minority among modern liberals believe that the very existence of armed forces, especially professional forces, is the primary cause of world conflict. They advocate an immediate unilateral disarmament. Another large and growing liberal element favors the increased use of available military power in non-traditional roles such as expanded domestic and international humanitarian assistance projects, and as a major contributor to United Nations peace keeping, and peace enforcement operations.

Modern conservatives, conversely, share the federalist conviction that to be effective, governments must possess an efficient, centralized military capability. They point to recent world events in Eastern Europe, the Persian Gulf , and South America, and dismiss liberal disarmament proposals as utopian and unrealistic. Many conservatives regard the government's obligation to provide for the common defense as among its most fundamental functions, and remain committed to funding a force structure adequate to meet immediate and potential threats.

They retain a strong commitment to maximize the military's professionalism and efficiency, and are generally skeptical that National Guard and Reserve forces can be maintained at a level of readiness sufficient for them to substitute for the regular establishment. Even were such readiness levels easily attainable, many regard the domestic political cost associated with mobilizing large numbers of Reserve forces for contingency operations as prohibitive.

Ironically, while they advocate larger overall force structures, many conservatives are far more reluctant to commit even regular U.S. forces to numerous overseas operations than are the liberals. In this regard they perpetuate the isolationist policies of the federalists. These conservatives adhere to a modern, stringent interpretation of the Washington doctrine as interpreted in the 20th century by Secretary of Defense Caspar Weinberger. This doctrine called for a commitment of U.S. Armed Forces only when the nations vital interests are unequivocally threatened.

Even then, according to Weinberger, the military should only be committed in overwhelming force to ensure a certainty of outcome, and only when a clearly definable, and achievable endstate had been determined. Since a confluence of these circumstances are comparatively rare, and because such operations are both economically, and politically expensive, such operations would be infrequently, and reluctantly undertaken.

These conservatives believe, as strongly as do the liberal pacifists, that the United States should not become further militarily entangled in the rapidly growing number of United Nations operations around the world. A small, but prominent minority of conservatives disagrees with the Weinberger philosophy and believes America should take a leading role in international peacekeeping, and even peace enforcement operations. These beliefs, however, cause this group to be even more skeptical of the the current Reserve organization's ability to meet the exigencies of such long-term, and domestically unpopular missions. They therefore advocate an even greater reliance upon a regular military establishment than their more isolationist compatriots.

2. <u>Attitude Towards the Relationship Between the Military and Society</u>:

Liberals continue to assert that the military must be representative of the parent society as a whole. In the modern debate, this conviction leads liberals to agitate for the repeal of gender restrictive combat policies, and to lift the ban on homosexuals in the Armed Services. These demands are part and parcel of the general goal to democratize the military and are made with little reference to the impact of such innovations on the military's efficiency or morale.

In this context, liberals view service in the Armed Forces as an employment opportunity materially equal to any other government job, and demand equal access to it across the demographic spectrum. They reject characterization of military service as "unique," and regard such arguments as dangerously elitist, and indicative of inherent negative cultural bias. Many liberals share the traditional republican concern that the societal loyalty of a military composed of too great a concentration from any one demographic group may begin to erode.

A substantial minority of liberals notes that black and underclass Americans are disproportionately represented in the military, and that society's inherent injustice forces such citizens to involuntarily hire themselves as mercenaries. They believe that the regular forces are, therefore, consciously or unconsciously repressive to the underclass. Many reject counter arguments to the effect that

157

minority opportunity in the military is demonstrably greater than in most civilian occupations as irrelevant. Since they regard military service as a marginal, last resort employment option, they believe minority success in the military merely obscures larger, and more pressing social justice issues.

Modern liberal antipathy to military service in general (except as a tool for advancing other social agendas as in the case of gay and women's rights) has all but eclipsed the traditional republican commitment to universal military service as a civic obligation. To the extent that this idea continues to be part of the debate, it has generally been expanded to include other government service options, such as the Peace Corps, Conservation Corps, or social welfare service as well. Nonetheless, elements of the debate remain, chief among them the preference for part-time citizen soldiers such as the National Guard because they are perceived to be less "militaristic."

A substantial amount of liberals, as well as conservatives remain skeptical, however, about the advisability of abandoning the draft and continuing with the All Volunteer Army experiment. Their objections stem from both ideological conviction and practical concerns. Ideologically they remain skeptical about the moral health of a society that demands no sacrifice from its citizens for its defense. Pragmatically, they are concerned that the continuing soundness of a volunteer army is subject to both the vagaries of the civilian economy and the social dynamics of the military's changing popularity as a profession. Notably, the 18th century republican notion that a major function of the military is to foster civic virtue by engaging in universal military service thus teaching the value of self-sacrifice, has, in the modern period, been absorbed by a substantial number of conservatives.

Most conservatives, however, retain the federalist conviction
that first and foremost, the military must be able to fulfill its
professional function. They regard military service as unique, and are
unconcerned with any demographic lopsidedness that may develop. Like
the federalists, these conservatives do not view the military itself as
a necessary reflection of society, but rather as an organizational
instrument of government power. The military's functional imperative,
therefore, is to maximize efficiency. Any social engineering, or
experimentation that disrupts the traditional organization, damages
morale, or otherwise detracts from the military's primary mission is
unacceptable to them.

3. Attitude Towards Military Preparedness:

Liberals, as did the republicans, object strenuously to the
massive portion of revenue devoted to defense. They regard these
expenditures as detracting from urgently needed funding for public
infrastructure and social programs. With the collapse of the Soviet
Union, many liberals fail to see any immediate compelling threat to
U.S. interests that requires the expenditure of even a fraction of the
current defense budget. They remain skeptical of the "deterrence"
policy and openly suspect that the evaluation of the current or
potential military threats to the U.S. have been exaggerated by the
military in order to maintain budgets at near Cold War levels. Most
liberals see no imperative to modernize equipment and are suspicious
that modernization programs are thinly veiled attempts to further the
military's own interests.

Many liberals believe that the United States' new status as the
world's sole superpower should allow her to reduce her military to all
but a token force. They argue that economic security is the gravest
threat currently confronting the Republic. In order to deal with this
threat they advocate a massive diversion of defense funds into domestic

159

economic programs, and a massive downsizing of the defense
establishment. This downsizing can be facilitated, they believe, by
an accelerated transfer of many active duty functions to the National
Guard and Reserves. They regard a sound American economy and
industrial base, combined with the moral authority gained by military
divestment, as providing the best future defense.

Conservatives are still convinced that a high degree of
military preparedness is the only credible way of continuing the
deterrence policy. They remain wedded to Washington's dictum that the
best way to maintain the peace is to prepare for war. Conservatives
believe that while large defense budgets seem extravagant, compared to
a crash rearmament campaign or actual war, they are comparatively
cheap. Furthermore, they note that massive cancellation of existing
defense contracts and the termination of major weapons modernization
programs will itself have a a significant negative impact on the
domestic economy.

Finally, their assessment of the continuing threats to world
peace and stability, combined with a desire to maintain America's
continuing international leadership, convince them that the United
States will probably be engaged in continuing low to mid level
conflicts for the foreseeable future. The United States must,
therefore, retain significant military forces in an immediate state of
preparedness and continue to back them up with substantial and highly
trained and equipped reserve forces.

The only dramatic omission from the 18th century list in these
modern debates is the absence of any serious consideration of the
wholesale disbandment of the regular forces in favor of their
replacement by the National Guard. This reflects the extent to which
the Federal Government and the regular military establishment have
successfully subordinated the autonomy of the state government and

160

militia to the Federal authority. Even so, echoes of this 18th century struggle can still be discerned in the continuing state challenges to total Federal control of the National Guard.

The ideological elements in the debates on downsizing and reorganizing the U.S. Armed Forces in the 1990s closely parallel those that animated the debates on the creation of a permanent American military establishment in the 1790s. These parallels demonstrate the extent to which these enduring ideologies continue to exert a profound influence on public and military attitudes towards the military establishment. A clear understanding of these influences is critical to anyone concerned with the outcome of these defense policy debates.

Since the demise of the Soviet Union, the historic American social pressure to maintain only a minimal military establishment has reasserted itself with growing force. The nearly 40 years of Cold War between the United States and the Soviet Union, that lasted from the beginning of the Korean War until the final collapse of the Soviet Empire in 1990, largely kept these pressures at bay. The clear and immediate threat posed by the Soviets, and the the frequent military confrontations between the two nations served to generate an American public opinion generally favorable to the maintenance of large regular and reserve establishments. In the absence of this clear threat, the historic divergence between republican and federalist defense theories is once again dominating the political debate.

The United States' position of international dominance since the Second World War, its current level of international economic involvement, and its political leadership act to complicate the historic ideological paradigm. The majority of both the liberal and conservative leadership expect, and sometimes demand that the United States stay fully engaged in world affairs, and thereby retain its position of international leadership. At the same time they expect that this can be accomplished with dramatically reduced forces, and budgets by acting in concert with foreign allies. The current trend in American defense policy is to engage in a rapidly increasing number of military operations around the world, such as in Iraq, Somalia, Korea, and Bosnia, but to do so with the minimum possible forces.[7]

In practice, events have demonstrated that the United States does not have clear legal precedents under which Congress will allow the Armed Forces to function as subordinate to an international coalition. Nor have the international umbrella organizations, such as the United Nations, created an administrative command and control apparatus capable of effectively managing such military operations. This means that in most cases where the United States becomes involved, it will continue to have to provide the vast majority of both logistic support and command and control capabilities.

Practice has also demonstrated that both the resources and time necessary to successfully accomplish such operations are usually badly underestimated. These policies, coinciding with the massive force reductions, reorganizations, and the curtailment or cancellation of numerous equipment procurement and modernization programs are placing a severe strain on the available resources of the regular military.

In order to cope with this strain, the regular military is forced to rely heavily upon the resources and manpower of the National Guard. An environment of diminished resources, however, exacerbates the traditional rivalry between the National Guard and Regular Army by forcing them to compete even more strenuously for the reduced funding available. This circumstance tends, as the debates enumerated in chapter six demonstrate, to reinforce the traditional ideological prejudices of both sides in the debate. Given the fact that the influence of these powerful ideas on key figures in the debate is often subconscious, an understanding of their historical and philosophical origin is essential if one hopes to separate dogma from objective reality. Failure to appreciate these influences is often starkly apparent.

The historical evidence indicates that too often, members of the professional military have argued for changes in the defense establishment from a narrow functional--institutional perspective with insuficient regard for the sociological and ideological imperatives that exert an equal, and sometimes greater influence on the issues. Failure frequently results in a bewildered cynicism, and a derisive dismissal of the opposition's motivations as "partisan" or "political." Members of the regular establishment oftimes fail to familiarize themselves with the tangled history of Regular Army and National Guard relationships, and are hence unprepared for the level of ingrained suspicion and hostility towards the regulars harbored by many Guard personnel. The regulars' frequent insensitivity to the complexities of the Guard's diverse relationships with the federal, state, and local authorities also poses a serious handicap to developing a more cooperative working relationship.

The Guard and Reserve, for their part, often fail to understand the differences in professional military standards that separates them from the regular forces. Their (historically justifiable) concern that they continue to receive adequate modern equipment and training funds oftimes forces them to exaggerate the realistic levels of military proficiency they can achieve with approximately 36 days of training per year. Their insistence, for ideological reasons, on being included as immediately deployable, fully combat ready forces diminishes their professional credibility in the eyes of the active-duty force.

Under limited circumstances exceptional Guard units might be able to achieve a deployable state of readiness for brief periods, but it is patently ridiculous to expect to maintain this state indefinitely. This incredulity, in turn, erodes the public's regard and respect for the Guard's honorable and vital function as the nation's partially trained combat reserves. This lack of public respect for the Guard's military abilities also can degrade their ability to perform their critical state support missions in that in any emergency, some critics are quick to exaggerate the Guard's slightest failing and urge their replacement with regular federal troops.

A key to breaking this cycle of exaggerated expectation, and self-fulfilling prophesy is a thorough and <u>objective</u> appreciation for the historical origins of the ideological prejudices. Armed with such understanding, any individual involved in the defense policy debates has a greatly enhanced probability of constructing proposals, and arguments best calculated to avoid ideological impasse. Furthermore, both the National Guard and the Regular Army are going to have to evolve a unified and effective strategy to cope with another major trend in civil-military relations, which is the resurgence of concern on the part of many special interest groups with the military's perceived lack of responsiveness to the core values of the American Creed.

In many ways, these core values, liberty, equality, individualism, democracy, and the rule of constitutional law, are, as was noted earlier, fundamentally incompatible with the military's functional-institutional imperatives. This fact was understood from the inception of American regular forces and was reflected in Congress' adoption of a separate set of military laws, the "Articles of War," intended to meet the unique demands of military life and discipline.

The existence of this separate military law and culture remained offensive to many republicans, and was a major source of their ideological objection to standing forces. Nevertheless, the basic rationale for the retention of a set of fundamentally repressive laws governing military personnel in active service went largely unchallenged for most of the 19th and 20th centuries. What legal challenges were mounted were nearly always decided by high courts in favor of the military.

Beginning in the early 1950's, however, the military has become increasingly influenced by American society's general trend towards an expanded emphasis on individual and civil rights. This influence first manifested itself in the decision to repeal the Articles of War as the legal code governing the Armed Forces, and to replace them with the Uniform Code of Military Justice which more closely approximated civilian legal codes. This action resulted, however, in a concomitant reduction in the disciplinary authority of junior officers and NCOs.

These influences were also demonstrated in the political pressures that led to desegregation of military units during the Korean War. During the Vietnam War, this movement, coupled with the general unpopularity of the war and the resurgence of strong republican ideology, resulted in major changes in American military culture. Regulations were revamped, and standards of living and the work environment were changed to more closely approximate civilian norms. Concurrent with the formation of the All Volunteer Force in the early 1970's, the role of women in the military was greatly expanded further changing traditional military culture.

The influence of American society's renewed emphasis on individual rights continues in the current legal and political battles over the issues of gays in the military, the assignment of women to combat roles, and Affirmative Action programs within the Armed Forces. The primary impetus behind these controversies stems from various special interest groups' desire to forward their own social agendas, but the relatively large base of support for these interest groups among the general population reflects a renewed and pervasive concern with the meaning of the American Creed within the context of regular military service.

The divisive nature of these issues is beginning to reawaken some of republicanism's traditional mistrust and suspicion of the military that has been largely dormant since the termination of the draft. Exacerbating this situation is the assumption of power by a new generation of American political leadership, many of whom have had no personal military service experience, and who's personal political ideologies were formed in the liberal social movements of the 1960's. These leaders exhibit in full measure the republican's traditional animosity to the military ethic, and an instinctive distrust of the motives and objectives of professional soldiers.

Increasingly, the military is going to have to contend with the basic issue which animated the republican/federalist debates, and continues to animate the conservative/liberal defense debate. That issue is how an effective military establishment can coexist within a society that values liberty and democracy above all else, and not pose a threat to the values of that society. The concerns expressed by a range of influential writers from Friar Drinan to Dr. Kohn demonstrate that, for a significant portion of liberal activists, this remains an immediate, important issue and not a mere intellectual abstraction.

Most fundamentally, the military needs to develop and maintain an appreciation for the historic events and circumstances which created this tension. They must then realize that justifying the military's role within society is going to remain a permanent obligation. The military is going to have to look critically at its own institutional conservatism and remain flexible enough to differentiate those elements in the military ethic which are fundamental and must be defended at all costs, from those which reflect transient cultural values such as, perhaps, demographic make-up.

The military's leadership must allow for the ideological prejudices of the nation's politics, and devise force structures and contingency plans which accomodate these inevitable concerns. This will require considerable compromise, and is guaranteed to result in solutions that are neither as efficient, nor as desireable as military planners would wish. They are going to have to devise strategies for comunicating to a Congress and Executive Branch that will be largely lacking personal military experience, without appearing to exercise an excessive, or unseemly political influence.

The regular military must expect that it will never receive all it calculates is required in the way of active-duty manpower and resources to adequately fulfill the myriad missions it will be assigned. The National Guard, for its part, is going to have to accept significant reductions and reorganizations in its future force structure if it hopes to retain a meaningful, credible, role within the Total Force concept.

Finally, all leaders must recognize the unique and complex relationship between American society, the professional military, and the citizen soldier. For the foreseeable future, the American military can confidently expect to be regarded by the civil society with that contradictory measure of respect and suspicion so confusing and disconcerting to many professional soldiers. Within the context of American democracy all policy will ultimately represent political compromise. In his work, American Politics: the Promise of Disharmony, Dr. Huntington summed up the phenomenon in this manner:

American history is the history of the efforts of groups to promote their interests by realizing American ideals. What is important, however, is not that they succeed but that they fail, not that the dream is realized but that it is not and can never be realized completely or satisfactorily. In the American context there will always be those who say that the institutional glass is half-empty and who will spill much passion attempting to fill it to the brim from the spring of idealism. But in the nature of things, particularly in America, it can never be much more than half-full.[8]

END NOTES

Chapter 1

[1]Lawrence D. Cress, "The Standing Army, The Militia, and the New Republic" (Doctoral Dissertation, University of Virginia, 1976), iii.

[2]Title 10 - Armed Forces, Chapter 13, para. 311. (b) (1), United States Code.

Chapter 2

[1]Most of the early colonies did hire military advisors, who were also members (and not simply employees) of the colony. Notable among these were Captains John Smith of Jamestown, and Miles Standish of Plymouth. Their military function was to organize and lead the colony's militia, not to serve as discretely professional soldiers.

[2]Allan R. Miller & Peter Maslowski, For The Common Defense (New York, 1984) 3.

[3]Douglas Edward Leach, Flintlock and Tomahawk (East Orleans, MA., 1958) 12-13.

[4]Ibid., 4.

[5]Patrick M. Malone, The Skulking Way of War (Baltimore, 1991) passim.

[6]David Ross Locke, A Letter To Bishop Mandell Creighton (London, 1887).

[7]Comte Jaques de Guibert, Essai General de Tactique (Liege, 1775) I, xiii, trans. Michael Howard, War in European History, (Oxford, 1976) 74.

[8]Charles C. Royster, A Revolutionary People At War (New York, 1980) Chapter 3 passim.

[9]Ibid.

[10]Richard M. Ketchum, <u>The Winter Soldiers</u> (New York, 1973) 177-178.

[11]Richard Palmer, <u>Early American Wars And Military Institutions</u> (Wayne,NJ, 1986) 45.

[12]George Washington to the Continental Congress, 17 January 1778, <u>Basic Writings Of George Washington</u>, ed. Saxe Commins (New York, 1948) 474.

[13]James K. Martin & Mark E. Lender, <u>A Respectable Army: The Military Origins Of the Republic, 1763-1789</u> (Arlington Hts., Ill., 1982) 202.

[14]Ibid. 186-194.

[15]Ibid. A popular expression to describe a useless, or valueless item was that it was "not worth a continental."

[16]Christopher & James L. Collier, <u>Decision In Philadelphia</u> (New York, 1986) 10.

[17]Lawrence D. Cress, <u>The Standing Army, the Militia, and the New Republic: Changing Attitudes about the Military in American Society</u>, (Dissertation, University of Virginia, 1976), 204.

[18]Colliers, <u>Decision in Philadelphia</u>, 20.

[19]Edward M. Burns, <u>James Madison: Philosopher Of The Constitution</u> (New Brunswick, NJ., 1938) 27.

[20]Collier, <u>Decision In Philadelphia</u>, 317.

[21]Richard H. Kohn, <u>Eagle and Sword</u> (New York, 1975) 13.

[22]Palmer, <u>Early American Wars</u>, 45-46.

[23]Jack J. Gifford, "One Nation . . . Making it Work," <u>Military Review</u>, LXVII No.9 (Sept. 1987) 18-21.

Chapter 3

[1]Edmund Burke, as quoted in: Michael Howard, <u>Soldiers and Governments</u> (London, 1957) III.

[2]<u>The American Heritage Dictionary</u> (Boston, 1982).

[3]Michael E. Hart, The 100. (New York, 1978) 261-263.

[4]Thomas Hobbes, As quoted in: Ibid., 262.

[5]Thomas Jefferson et. al., "The Declaration of Independence" (Philadelphia, 1776).

[6]Trevor Clobourn, The Lamp of Experience (Chapel Hill, 1965) App. II.

[7]Ibid., 185.

[8]Ibid., Chapter 3 passim.

[9]Ibid., 185.

[10]Howard, Soldiers and Governments, 170.

[11]Charles Rollin, The Ancient History (Boston, 1827) As quoted in: Colbourn, The Lamp of Experience, 22.

[12]Ibid.

[13]Colbourn, The Lamp of Experience, 23.

[14]Ibid., 23-24.

[15]Oliver Goldsmith, The Roman History (London, 1771) As quoted in: Goldwin Smith, A History of England, (New York, 1949) 462.

[16]Colbourn, The Lamp of Experience, 23-24.

[17]John Trenchard & Thomas Gordon, Cato's Letters (London, 1724) As quoted in: Smith, A History of England, 465.

[18]Alexander Hamilton, et. al. The Federalist Papers ed. Garry Wills (Boston, 1982) Introduction passim.

[19]Paul L. Ford, Pamphlets on the Constitution of the United States (New York, 1968) Introduction passim.

[20]John Jay, "The Federalist No. 5," The Federalist Papers, 18.

[21]Reginal C. Stuart, "Engines of Tyranny: Recent Historiography on Standing Armies During the Era of the American Revolution." The Canadian Journal of History no. 10 (October 1990) 183-97.

[22] Smith, <u>A History of England</u>, 301.

[23] Fay Franklin, <u>Hstory's Timeline</u> (New York, 1981) 136.

[24] John Keegan et. al., <u>Who's Who in Military History</u> (London, 1976) 83.

[25] Franklin, <u>History's Timeline</u>, 137.

[26] Colbourn, <u>The Lamp of Experience</u>, 11.

[27] Ibid.

[28] Edmund Ludlow, <u>Memoirs of Edmund Ludlow</u> (London, 1699) As Quoted in: Colbourn, <u>The Lamp of Experience</u>, 44.

[29] George F. Sheer et. al., <u>Rebels and Redcoats</u> (Cleveland, 1957) 136.

[30] John Trenchard, and Thomas Gordon, <u>Cato's Letters, or Essays on Liberty, Civil and Religious and Other Important Subjects</u>. As Quoted In : John Todd White, "Standing Armies In Time of War: Republican Theory and Practice During the American Revolution." (Doctoral Dissertation: George Washington University, 1978) 40.

[31] Samuel Adams, <u>The Writings of Samuel Adams</u> 11 vols., ed. William Forte (Chicago, 1947) VII. 220.

[32] Thomas Jefferson, <u>Papers of Thomas Jefferson</u> 17 vols. (Princeton, 1950) II, 195-198.

[33] James Flexner, <u>Washington: the Indispensable Man</u> (New York, 1969) 67.

[34] Sheer, <u>Rebels and Redcoats</u>, 94.

[35] Ibid.

[36] George A, Billias, <u>Elbridge Gerry: Founding Father & Republican Statesman</u> (New York, 1976) 76.

[37] Don Higgenbotham, <u>George Washington and the American Military Tradition</u> (Athens, GA., 1985.) 50.

[38] James K. Martin & Mark E. Lender, <u>A Respectable Army: the Military Origins of the Republic, 1763-1789</u> (Arlington Hts, 1982) 72-94.

[39] John Adams, "Letter to Joseph Hawley," 1776, As Quoted In : White, _Standing Armies In Time of War_, 182.

[40] George Washington, _Letter to Lund Washington, 1776_, As Quoted In: Flexner, _Washington: the Indispensable Man_, 84.

[41] Martin & Lender, _A Respectable Army_, 96-102.

[42] _The Encyclopedia of National Biography: From Earliest Times to 1915_, 42 vols. (Oxford. 1953) VII. 782-785.

[43] Flexner, _Washington : the Indispensable Man_, 80-87. See Also: Ketchum, _The Winter Soldiers: The Battles for Trenton and Princeton_. (New York, 1973) Chapter 4. Offers a convincing case for conspiracy; John Shy, _A People Numerous and Armed_ (Ann Arbor, 1990) 135-162., Offers and excellent analysis of Lee's Character.

[44] Francis W, Greene, _The Revolutionary War and the Military Policy of the United States_. (Port Washington NY. 1911) 293.

[45] George Washington, "Letter to the Continental Congress," December 20, 1776, As Quoted In : Ibid.

[46] George Washington, "Letter to Continental Congress," 24 September, 1776, As Quoted In: Ibid.

[47] Don Higgenbotham, _War and Society in Revolutionary America: the Wider Dimensions of Conflict_ (Columbia, 1988) 114.

[48] Ibid.

[49] Ibid., 115.

[50] White, _Standing Armies In Time of War_, 181.

[51] Ibid.

[52] Peter Karsten, _The Military In America_ (New York, 1986) Chapter 8 provides a study of the careers of 50 continental officers from Pennsylvania.

[53] Bill Mauldin, _Up Front_. (New York, 1945) Introduction passim.

[54] Sheer, _Rebels and Redcoats_, 500 - 501.

[55] Howard, _Soldiers and Governments_, 12.

CHAPTER 4

[1]Richard H. Kohn, Eagle and Sword (New York, 1975) 40-42.

[2]George Washington, "Sentiments On A Peace Establishment", report to the Continental Congress, May 1783, Basic Writings of George Washington, ed. Saxe Commins (New York, 1948) 467-487.

[3]Ibid.

[4]Ibid.

[5]Ibid.

[6]Ibid.

[7]Ibid.

[8]Ibid.

[9]Lawerence D. Cress, "The Standing Army, the Militia, and the New Republic: Changing Attitudes About the Military in American Society," (Doctoral Dissertation, University of Virginia, 1976) 204.

[10]George Washington, "Circular to the States," April 1783, Basic Writings of George Washington, 489-495.

[11]Ibid.

[12]Ibid.

[13]Kohn, Eagle and Sword, 41.

[14]Cress, "The Standing Army, the Militia, and the New Republic: Changing Attitudes About the Military in American Society," 222-225.

[15]Ibid.

[16]George Washington, "Observations on a Peace Establishment," October 1783, Writings of George Washington, ed. Worthington C. Ford, 15 vols. (New York, 1891) X, 315.

[17]Cress, "The Standing Army, the Militia, and the New Republic: Changing Attitudes About the Military in American Society," 224.

[18]Charles W. Royster, The Continental Army in the American Mind: 1775-1783, (Doctoral Dissertation, The University of California, Berkeley, 1977) 590-592.

[19]Ibid.

[20]Ibid.

[21]Ibid.

[22]James K. Martin and Mark E. Lender, A Respectable Army: the Military Origins of the Republic, 1763-1789, (Arlington Hts., Ill., 1982) 197.

[23]Cress, "The Standing Army, the Militia, and the New Republic: Changing Attitiudes About the Military in American Society," 225.

[24]Royster, "The Continental Army in the American Mind: 1775-1783," 571-574.

[25] Lawerence D. Cress, Citizens In Arms: the Army and the Militia in American Society to the War of 1812, (Chapel Hill, N.C., 1983) 68-69.

[26]Ibid.

[27]Royster, "The Continental Army in the American Mind: 1775-1783," 566-568.

[28]Ibid.

[29]Arthur St. Clair, Letter, 1783, As quoted in: Royster, "The Continental Army in the American Mind: 1775-1783," 567.

[30]Cress, Citizens In Arms, 70.

[31]Anonymous Pamphlet, As quoted in; Royster, "The Continental Army in the American Mind: 1775-1783," 569.

[32]Ibid., 570.

[33]Ibid.

[34]Ibid.

[35]Letter to the Editor, The Gazzette of the United States, 1783, As quoted in: Ibid.

[36]Cress, "The Standing Army, the Militia, and the New Republic: Changing Attitiudes About the Military in American Society," 226.

[37]Martin and Lender, A Respectable Army, 204.

[38]Royster, "The Continental Army in the American Mind: 1775-1783," 573-574.

[39]Ford, The Writings of George Washington, 388.

[40]Thomas Jefferson, Letter to George Washington, February 1784, The Writings of George Washington, 387-388.

[41]Ibid., 389.

[42]Thomas Jefferson, As quoted in: Royster, "The Continental Army in the American Mind: 1775-1783," 582.

[43]Martin and Lender, A Respectable Army, 206.

[44]Ibid.

[45]Elbridge Gerry, As quoted in: George A. Billias, Elbridge Gerry: Founding Father And Republican Statesman (New York, 1977) 111-112.

[46]Ibid.

[47]Ibid.

[48]James Lowell, As quoted in: Cress, Citizens in Arms, 68.

[49]Martin and Lender, A Respectable Army, 202.

[50]William R. Smith, History as Argument: Three Patriot Historians of the American Revolution (the Hague, 1966) 34-39.

[51]Ibid.

[52]Walter Millis, Arms And Men (New York, 1956) 47.

[53]Christopher and James L. Collier, Decision in Philadelphia (New York, 1986) 321.

[54]Thomas Hobbes, as quoted in: Michael Howard, Soldiers and Governments (London, 1957) VIII.

[55]Ibid., 312-331.

[56]Ibid.

[57]The Constitution of the United States, Article I, Section 8.

[58]Colliers, Decision In Philadelphia, 322.

[59]John K. Mahon, The American Militia: Decade of Decision, 1789-1800 (Monograph, University of Florida, Gainesville, 1960) 10.

[60]Colliers, Decision In Philadelphia, 322.

[61]Billias, Elbridge Gerry, 167.

[62]The Constitution of the United States, Article I, Section 8.

[63]Colliers, Decision In Philadelphia, 341.

[64]Morten Borden, The Anti-Federalist Papers (Michigan State, 1965) viii.

[65]Ibid.

[66]Dumas Malone, Jefferson and the Rights of Man (Boston, 1951) 173.

[67]Alexander Hamilton, "Federalist No. 8," The Federalist Papers, 32.

[68]Ibid.

[69]Patrick Henry, "Pamphlet on the Federal Constitution; 1788," The Anti-Federalist Papers, 11-22.

[70]James Wilson, "A Speech on the Constitution," Pamphlets on the Constitution of the United States: 1787-1788, ed. Paul L. Ford (Brooklyn, N.Y., 1888) 157-158.

[71]Elbridge Gerry, Observations on the Proposed Constitution, As quoted in: Ibid.,10.

[72]Noah Webster, Examination of the Proposed Federal Constitution, As quoted in : Ibid., 152.

[73]Brutus, "Objections to a Standing Army Part I," The Anti-Federalist Papers, 63.

[74]Brutus, "Objections to a Standing Army Part II," Ibid., 66.

[75]Ibid., 67.

[76]See pamphlets of Patrick Henry, George Clinton, or Robert Yates, all of whom make this allegation in one form or another.

[77]"The Articles of Confederation of the United States," Article II, Decision in Philadelphia, Appendix I.

[78]James Madison, "Federalist No.14," The Federalist Papers, 62.

[79]Cress, "The Standing Army, the Militia, and the New Republic: Changing Attitiudes About the Military in American Society,", 245.

[80]Alexander Hamilton, "Federalist No. 24," The Federalist Papers, 116.

[81]Ford, Pamphlets on the Constitution, vi.

[82]Colliers, Decision In Philadelphia, 349.

[83]Ibid., 341.

[84]Kohn, Eagle and Sword, 86.

[85]Ibid., 82.

[86]Martin and Lender, A Respectable Army, 172.

[87]Samuel P. Huntington, American Politics: The Promise Of Disharmony (Cambridge, MA., 1981) 12.

[88]Alexander Hamilton, "Federalist No.6," The Federalist & Other Constitutional Papers, ed. E.H. Scott (Chicago, 1898) 78.

[89]Borden, The Anti-Federalist Papers, x.

[90]Huntington, American Politics, 15.

Chapter 5

[1]James Ripley Jacobs, The Beginings of the U.S. Army: 1783--1812 (Princeton, Princeton University Press, 1947) 43.

[2]George Washington, "Address to Congress," August 7, 1789, As quoted in: John MacAuley Palmer, America in Arms (New Haven, Yale Press, 1941) 38-39.

[3]George Washington, Personal Diary (Entry for December 18, 1789) As quoted in: Ibid., 39.

[4]George Washington, Personal Diary (Entry for December 19, 1789) As quoted in: Ibid., 40.

[5]Ibid.

[6]James Madison, "Letter to Thomas Jafferson", January 24, 1790, As quoted in: Irving Bryant, James Madison: The Nationalist (New York, Bob-Merril Inc., 1948) 272.

[7]Palmer, America in Arms, 43.

[8]Ibid., 44.

[9]Editorial, The Gazette of the United States, As quoted in: Ibid., 44.

[10]Benjamin Lincoln, "Letter to Henry Knox," February 7, 1790, As quoted in: North Callahan, Henry Knox (New York, Rivehart, 1958) 271.

[11]John K. Mahon, The American Militia: Decade of Decision 1789-1800 (Gainesville, Univ. of Florida Press, 1960) 15-17.

[12]Jacobs, The Beginings of the U.S. Army, 45.

[13]Mahon, The American Militia, 15.

[14]Palmer, America in Arms, 52.

[15]Ibid., 17.

[16]Mahon, The American Militia, 17-18.

[17]Jacobs, The Beginings of the U.S. Army, 46.

[18]Editorial, The National Gazette, May 8, 1792, As quoted in: Ibid., 53.

[19]Ibid.

[20]Mahon, The American Militia, 20.

[21]Palmer, America in Arms, 44.

[22]William Maclay, "Statement in Congress," May 13, 1792, As quoted in: Jacobs, The Beninings of the U.S. Army, 46.

[23]Richard H. Kohn, Eagle and Sword (New York, McMillian, 1975) 109.

[24]Dave R. Palmer and James W. Stryker, _Early American Wars and Military Institutions_, "West Point Historical Series," ed, Thomas E. Griess (Wayne,N.J.,1986) 46.

[25]Mahon, _The American Militia_, 18.

[26]Ibid.

[27]Kohn, _Eagle and Sword_, 132.

[28]Jacobs, _The Beginings of the U.S. Army_, 192.

[29]Kohn, _Eagle and Sword_, 137-138.

[30]Ibid., 224.

[31]Jacobs, _The Beginqings of the U.S. Army_, 268.

[32]Leonard D. White, _The Jeffersonians_ (New York, Miflin, 1951) 212.

[33]Henry Dearborn, "Letter to Thomas Jefferson," October 8, 1798, As quoted in: Kohn, _Eagle and Sword_, 138.

[34]Ibid., 301.

Chapter 6

[1]Robert F. Drinan, "Military establishment threatens U.S. democracy," _National Catholic Reporter_, 29 October 1993, 12.

[2]Ibid.

[3]Samuel P. Huntington, _American Politics: The Promise of Disharmony_ (Cambridge, Harvard University Press, 1981) 237.

[4]Walter Milis, _Arms and Men_ (New Brunswick, N.J., Rutgers University Press, 1956) 214-218.

[5]Francis Vinton Greene, _The Military Policy of the United States_ (Port Washington, N.Y., Kennikat Press Inc., 1911) 316.

[6]Allan R. Millett & Peter Maslowski, _For The Common Defense_ (New York, Macmillian, 1984) 312-313.

[7]Ibid., 314.

[8]Robert K. Wright, Jr., and Renee Hylton Greene, A Brief History of the Militia and National Guard (Washington D.C.: National Guard Bureau, Office of Public Affairs, 1986) 27.

[9]John MacAuley Palmer, America in Arms (New Haven, Yale University Press, 1941) 121.

[10]Milis, Arms and Men, 214.

[11]Wodrow Wilson, "Annual Address to Congress, December 1914," As quoted in: Ibid., 215.

[12]Ibid., 215-217.

[13]Ibid., 218.

[14]Wright and Greene, A Brief History of the Militia and National Guard, 27.

[15]Lindley Garrison, "Letter to Wodrow Wilson, January 12, 1916," As quoted in: Milis, Arms and Men, 220.

[16]Wright and Greene, A Brief History of the Militia and National Guard, 27.

[17]Milis, Arms and Men, 236.

[18]Ibid.

[19]Eliot A. Cohen, Citizens and Soldiers: the Dilemmas of Military Service, (Ithaca, N.Y., Cornell University Press, 1985) 125-126.

[20]Michael Howard, War and the Liberal Conscience (New Brunswick, N.J. Rutgers University Press, 1978) 31.

[21]Ibid.

[22]Harry A. Harmion, The Case Against A Volunteer Army, (Chicago, Quadrangle Books, 1971) Introduction passim.

[23]Ibid., 34-35.

[24]Ibid., 61.

[25]T. R. Fehrenbach, This Kind of War (New York, Macmillan, 1963) 639.

[26]Davis B, Marlowe, "The Manning of the Force and Structure for Battle," <u>Conscripts and Volunteers</u>, ed. Robert K. Fullinwider (College Park, MD., Rowen and Allenheld Inc., 1983) 24-25.

[27]John W. Finney, "Letter to the New York Times, August 15, 1972," As quoted in: Sue E. Berryman, <u>Who Serves: The Persistent Myth of the Underclass Army</u> (Boulder, CO., Westview Press, 1988) 56.

[28]Shirley Chisolm, "Testimony Before the House Armed Services Committee, April 1970," As quoted in: Ibid., 59.

[30]George Bush, "The Soviet Bear Might Be Dead, but Wolves Still Stalk the World," <u>National Guard Magazine</u>, October 1992, 4.

[31]Bill Clinton, "Strengthening the Guard in the Total Force," Ibid., 6.

[32]Brian J. Boquist, "Why TLAT?" Ibid., 30-33.

[33]Editorial, <u>Los Angeles Times</u>, 26 November 1991, B6.

[34]William Pfaff, "Does America Want to Lead by Intimidation?'" <u>L.A. Times</u> (March 11, 1992) C8.

[35]Editorial, "Square One," <u>The New Republic</u>, 27 April 1992. 7.

[36]Patrick J. Buchanan, "America First--and Second, and Third," <u>The National Interest</u>, Spring 1990, 80.

[37]Editorial, "American Readiness," <u>L.A. Times</u>, 23 February 1992, M4.

[38]Samuel J. Newland, 'The National Guard: State versus National Control," <u>Public Administration Review</u>, January/February 1989, 68.

[39]Ibid., 71.

[40]Bruce Jacobs, Interview with the author, Washington D.C., 21 December 1993, Notes in possession of author.

[41]Bruce Jacobs, "Let the Buck Stop Here--In State Service," <u>National Guard Magazine</u>, October 1992, 46.

[42]Editorial, "Tomorrow the World," <u>The Progressive</u>, May 1992, 8.

[43]William Greider, "The Country that Stayed Out in the Cold," <u>Rolling Stone</u>, 23 January 1992, 19.

[44]Robert L. Borosage, "Defensive About Defense Cuts," The Nation, 9 March 1992, 1.

[45]Ibid.

[46]Robert L. Borosage, "Mugged Again," The Nation, 11 May 1992, 616- 617.

[47]George Bush, "Remarks to the National Guard association in Salt Lake City, Utah: September 15, 1992," Weekly Compilation of Presidential Documents (IWCP) vol.28, Iss: 38, 21 September 1992, 1656.

[48]Carl Conetta and Charles Knight, "Exaggerated Defense Threats," Letter to the Editors, The Washington Post, 30 September 1993, A15.

[49]Editorial, "The Week," National Review, 1 March 1993, 10.

[50]Paul W. Kahn, "Love Field," The New Republic, 8 March 1993, 19.

[51]Scott Shuger, "American Inquisition," The New Republic, 7 December 1992, 23.

[52] David R. Carlin, Jr., "Bishops & Generals," Commonweal, 15 January 1993, 10.

[53]David Horrowitz, "The Feminist Assault on the Military," National Review, 5 October 1992, 49.

[54]Ibid., 47.

[55]E.L. Patullo, "Why Not Gays in the Military?" National Review, March 1993, 41.

[56]Art Pine, "Military Haunted by a Paper Tiger," L.A. Times, 13 June 1993, A24.

[57]John Isaacs, "A Billion Dollar Bonanza," The Bulletin of Atomic Scientists, July/August 1993, 3-4.

[58]James F. Jacobs, The Beginnings of the U.S. Army: 1783-1812 (Princeton, N.J., Princeton University Press, 1947) 245.

[59]U.S. Army, Field Manual 100-5, "Operations," Washington D.C. Department of the Army, 1993. 13-4/13-8.

[60]Ibid.

[61]Article, "Kelly Requests National Guard to Police District," The Washington Post, 21 October 1993, A1.

[62]Editorial, "Let the Guard guard," L.A. Times, 27 October 1993, A26.

[63]Barbara Boxer, "Border Help," Letter to the Editors, L.A. Times, 5 November 1993, B8.

[64]Joseph D. McNamara, "Can you protect and serve and kill the enemy?" L.A. Times, 31 October 1993, M1.

[65]Harry G. Summers, Jr., "And Don't Forget That Armies Are Primarily For Fighting Wars," L.A. Times, 19 September 1993, B10.

[66]Ibid.

[67]Charles E. Heller, Twenty-First Century Force: A Federal Army and a Militia, Strategic Studies Institute, U.S. Army War College (Carlisle Barracks, PA., June 14, 1993) viii.

[68]Ibid., x.

[69]Ibid., xi.

[70]Ibid., x.

[71]Martin Binkin and William W. Kaufman, U.S. Army Guard & Reserve: Rhetoric, Realities, Risks (Washington D.C., Brookings Institution, 1989) Introduction passim.

[72]Ibid., 32.

[73]Jacobs, Interview with Author, 21 December 1993.

[74]Heller, Twenty-First Century Force, 10-35.

[75]Deborah R. Lee, "On the 20th Anniversary, Total Force is Real and No Longer a Concept," Reserve Officers Asociation, National Security Report (Washington D.C., Reserve Officers Association) September 1993, 29-30.

[76]Gordon R. Sullivan, "The Army Team = Trained and Ready," Video briefing presented to the United States Army Command And General Staff College, August 10, 1993, Ft. Leavenworth, KS.

[77]Bruce Reimer, Remarks to the U.S. Army Command And General Staff College students, January 5, 1994, Ft. Leavenworth, KS. Notes in possession of Author.

[78]Ibid.

[79]Ibid.

[80]Charles Dunlap, Jr., "The Origins of the American Military Coup of 2012," Parameters, Journal of the U.S. Army War College (Carlisle, PA.) April 1993, 29.

[81]Ibid.

[82]Ibid.

[83]Harry G. Summers, Jr., "Roots of the Coup of 2012 lie in 1992," L.A. Times, 2 December 1992, B7.

[84]David Corn, "A Very U.S. Coup," The Nation, 5 April 1993, 440.

[85]Richard H. Kohn, "Upstarts in Uniform," The New York Times, 10 April 1994, E3.

[86]Ibid.

Chapter 7

[1]Michael Howard, Soldiers and Governments (London, 1957) 169.

[2]Samuel P. Huntington, The Soldier and the State (Cambridge, 1959) 144.

[3]Ibid., 145.

[4]Samuel P. Huntington, American Poitics (Cambridge, 1981) 13-14.

[5]Ibid.

[6]Ibid., 237.

[7]Gordon R. Sullivan and James M. Dubik, "Land Warfare in the 21st Century," Military Review, vol. LXXIII (September, 1993) No. 9, 13-32 passim.

[8]Huntington, American Politics, 11-12.

BIBLIOGRAPHY

Books

Berryman, Sue E. Who Serves?: The Persistent Myth of the Underclass
    Army. Boulder, CO.: Westview Press. 1988.

Billias, George A. Elbridge Gerry: Founding Father and Republican
    Statesman. New York: McGraw-Hill Book Co. 1976.

Burns, Edward M. James Madison: Philosopher of the Constitution. New
    Brunswick, NJ.: Princeton College Press. 1938.

Brant, Irving, James Madison: The Nationalist 1780-1787. New York: The
    Bobbs-Merril Co. 1948.

_____. James Madison: Father of the Constitution 1787-1800. New
    York: The Bobbs - Merril Co. 1950.

Callahan, North, Henry Knox: General Washington's General. New York
    Rinehart & Co. 1958.

Colbourn, H. Trevor, The Lamp of Experience: Whig History and the
    Intellectual Origins of the American Revolution. Chapel Hill:
    University of North Carolina Press. 1965.

Collier, Christopher and J.L. Collier, Decision in Philadelphia. New
    York: Ballantine. 1986.

Cooper, Jerry, The Militia and National Guard in America Since Colonial
    Times. Westport, CT.: Greenwood Press. 1993.

Cress, Lawrence D. Citizens in Arms. Chapel Hill: University of North
    Carolina Press. 1982.

Culiffe, Marcus, Soldiers & Civilians. New York: Collier Macmillan.
    1973.

Flexner, James T. Washington: The Indispensable Man. New York: New
    American Library. 1984.

Franklin, Fay, History's Timeline. London: Grieswood & Dempsey Ltd.
    1981.

Greene, Francis V. The Revolutionary War and The Military Policy of The
    United States. New York: Charles Scribbners & Sons. 1911.

Hart, Michael H. The 100: A Ranking of the Most Influential Persons In History. New York: Galahad Books. 1978.

Heller, Charles E. and William A. Stofft, Americas First Battles 1776-1965. University Press of Kansas. 1986.

Hickey, Donald R. The War OF 1812. Urbana and Chicago: University of Illinois Press. 1989.

Higgenbotham, Don, War and Society in Revolutionary America: The Wider Dimensions of Conflict. Columbia: University of South Carolina Press. 1988.

_____. George Washington and the American Military Tradition. Athens, University of Georgia Press. 1985.

Howard, Michael, War and the Liberal Conscience. New Brunswick, N.J.: Rutgers University Press. 1978.

_____. Soldiers and Governments: Nine Studies in Civil-Military Relations. London: Eyre& Spottiswoode. 1957.

Huntington, Samuel P. American Politics: The Promise of Disharmony. Cambridge, MA.: Harvard University Press. 1981.

_____. The Soldier and the State. Cambridge, MA.: Harvard University Press. 1957.

Jacobs, James Ripley, The Beginning of the U.S. Army 1783-1812. Princeton, NJ.: Princeton University Press. 1947.

Karsten, Peter, The Military in America. New York: The Free Press. 1986.

Kaufman, William W. The McNamara Strategy. New York: Harper & Row.1964.

Ketchum, Richard M. The Winter Soldiers. New York: Doubleday. 1973.

Kohn, Richard H. Eagle and Sword. New York: Collier McMillan. 1975.

Leach, Douglas Edward, Flintlock and Tomahawk. East Orleans: Parnassus Press. 1958.

Lynn, Kenneth S. A Divided People. Westport, CT.: Greenwood Press. 1977.

Mahon, John K. The War Of 1812. New York: Da Capo Press. 1972.

Malone, Dumas, Jefferson and the Rights of Man. v.II. Boston: Little Brown & Co. 1951.

Malone, Patrick M. _The Skulking Way of War_. Baltimore: Johns Hopkins
    University Press. 1991.

Martin, James K. and Mark E. Lender. _A Respectable Army: The Military_
    Origins of the Republic, 1763-1789. Arlington Heights: Harlan
    Davidson Inc. 1982.

McKenna, George, _American Populism_. New York: G.P. Putnam's Sons. 1974.

Millet, Allan R. and PeterMaslowski. _For the Common Defense_. New York:
    Collier McMillan. 1984.

Minar, David W. _Ideas and Politics: The American Experience_. Homewood,
    Ill.: The Dorsey Press. 1964.

Preston, Richard A.& Sydney F. Wise, _Men in Arms_. New York: Holt,
    Rinehart And Winston. 1979.

Palmer, Dave R. and James W. Stryker, _Early American Wars and Military_
    Institutions. Wayne, N. J.: Avery Publishing Group. 1986.

Palmer, John Mcauley, _America In Arms_. New Haven: Yale University
    Press. 1941.

Royster, Charles C. _A Revolutionary People At War_. New York: Scribners
    & Sons. 1980.

Sheer, George F., and Hugh F. Rankin, _Rebels & Redcoats_. Cleaveland:
    World Publishing Co. 1957

Shy, John, _A People Numerous and Armed_. Ann Arbor: The University of
    Michigan Press. 1990.

Smith, Richard N. _Patriarch_. Boston: Houghton Mifflin Co. 1993.

Stagg, J. C. A. _Mr. Madison's War: Politics, Diplomacy, and Warfare in_
    the Early Republic, 1783 - 1830. Princeton, N.J.: Princeton
    University Press. 1983.

White, Leonard D. _The Jeffersonians_. New York: Houghton Mifflin Co.
    1952.

_____. _The Federalists_. New York: Houghton Mifflin Co. 1947.

Articles

Boquist, Brian J. "Why TLAT?'" _National Guard Magazine_, October 1992,
    30-33.

Borosage, Brian J. "Mugged Again," _The Nation_, 11 May 1992, 616-
    617.

Boxer, Barbara. "Border Help," L.A. Times, 5 November 1993, B8.

Buchanan, Patrick J. "America First- and Second, and Third," The National Interest, Spring 1990, 80.

Bush, George. "The Soviet Bear Might Be Dead, But Wolves Still Stalk the Land." National Guard Magazine, October 1992, 4.

Carlin, David R. Jr. "Bishops & Generals," Commonweal, 15 January 1993, 10.

Clinton, Bill. "Strengthening the Guard in the Total Force," National Guard Magazine, October 1992, 6.

Conetta, Carl, & Charles Knight, " Exaggerated Defense Threats," The Washington Post, 30 September 1993, A15.

Corn, David. "A Very U.S. Coup," The Nation, 5 April 1993, 440.

Drinan, Robert F. "Military Establishment Threatens U.S. Democracy." National Catholic Reporter, 29 October 1993, 12.

Dunlap, Charles Jr. " The Origins of the American Military Coup of 2012," Parameters, Journal of the U.S. Army War College, April 1993, 9.

Gifford, Jack J. "One Nation . . . Making it Work." Military Review. vol. LXVII. No.9. Leavenworth KS. US Army Command and General Staff College, September 1987, 14 -23.

Greider, William. "The Country that Stayed Out in the Cold," Rolling Stone, 23 January 1992, 19.

Horrowitz, David. " The Feminist Assault on the Military," National Review, 5 October 1992, 49.

Isaacs, John. "A Billion Dollar Bonanza," The Bulletin of Atomioc Scientists, July/August 1993, 3-4.

Jacobs, Bruce. "Tensions Between the Army National Guard and the Regular Army." Military Review. vol.LXXIII. No. 10 Leavenworth KS. US Army Command and Staff College, October 1993, 5-17.

_____. "Let the Buck Stop Here--In State Service," National Guard Magazine, October 1992, 46.

Kahn, Paul W. "Love Field," The New Republic, 8 March 1993, 19.

Kohn, Richard H. "Upstarts In Uniform," The New York Times, 11 April 1994, E3.

Lee, Deborah R. "On the 20th Anniversary, Total Force is Real and No Longer a Concept," <u>Reserve Officers Asociation, National Security Report</u>. (Washington D.C., Reserve Officers Association, September 1993, 29-30.

McNamara, Joseph D. "Can you protect and serve and kill the enemy?" <u>L.A. Times</u>, 31 October 1993, M1.

Marlowe, Davis H. "T   nning of the Force and Structure for Battle." <u>Conscripts and   nteers</u>. ed. Robert F. Fullinwider. College Park, MD., Rowen and Allenheld Inc. 1983.

Newland, Samuel J. "The National Guard: State versus National Control," <u>Public Administration Review</u>, January/February 1989, 68.

Pfaff, William. "Does America Want to Lead by Intimidation?'" <u>L.A. Times</u>, 11 March 1992, C8.

Patullo, E.L. "Why Not Gays in the Military?" <u>National Review</u>, March 1993, 41.

Pine, Art. "Military Haunted by a Pa   ger," <u>L.A. Times</u>, 13 June 1993, A24.

Shuger, Scott. "American Inquisition," <u>The New Republic</u>, 7 December 1992, 23.

Stuart, Reginald C. "Engines of Tyranny: Recent Historiography on Standing Armies During the Era of the American Revolution." <u>Canadian Journal of History</u>, October 1990, 183 -197.

Summers, Harry G. Jr. "Roots of the Coup of 2012 lie in 1992," <u>L.A.Times</u>, 2 December 1992, B7.

_____. "And Don't Forget That Armies Are Primarily For Fighting Wars," <u>L.A. Times</u>, 19 September 1993, B10.

Wooder, Chrles F. "Charles Lee." <u>Encyclopedia of National Biography</u> v.VII: 785-788.

Unpublished Dissertations, Theses, and Papers

Cress, Lawrence D. "The Standing Army, The Militia, And the New Republic: Changing Attitudes Toward the Military in American Society 1768-1820." (Doctoral Disseratation. University of Virginia, 1976.

Heller, Charles E. "Twenty-First Century Force: A Federal Army and a Militia." Report for the Strategic Studies Institute U.S. Army War College, 1993.

Jacobs, Bruce, Major General (Ret.) U.S. Army National Guard. 1993. Interview by author, 21 December, Washington, D.C., written notes, The Historical Society of the Militia and National Guard. Washington.

Kaune, Charles S. "The National Gaurd in War: An HIstorical Analysis of the 27th Infantry Division in World War II." Masters of Military Arts and Sciences, Thesis, U.S. Army Command and Staff College, 1990.

Mahon, John K. "The American Militia--Decade of Decision, 1789-1800." Monograph. University of Florida, Gainesville, 1960.

Royster, Charles W. "The Continental Army in the American Mind: 1775-1783." Doctoral Dissertation, University of California, Berkeley, 1977.

White, John Todd, "Standing Armies in Time of War: Republican Theory and Military Practice During the American Revolution." Doctoral Dissertation. George Washington University, 1978.

Wright, Robert K., Jr., "A Brief History of the Militia and National Guard." Report prepared for the Office of Public Affairs, National Guard Bureau, 1986.

Published Collections of Source Documents

Borden, Morten, The Anti-Federalist Papers. Ann Arbor: Michigan State University Press. 1965.

Commins, Saxe, The Basic Writings of George Washington. New York: Random House. 1948.

Ford, Paul Leicester, Pamphlets on the Constitution of the United States. New York: Da Capo Press. 1968.

Ford, Worthington Chauncey, The Writings of George Washington. New York: Putnam's Sons. 1891.

Hamilton, Alexander, et al., The Federalist and Other Constitutional Papers. ed. E. H. Scott. Chicago: Scott, Foresman & Co. 1898.